How You Can Be Led by the

Spirit
of
God

LEGACY EDITION

Provided by
Kingdom Empowerment ministries
Website: kemkitomorgan.weebly.com
Email: kito_morgan@yahoo.com

How You Can Be Led by the
Spirit *of* God

LEGACY EDITION
Expanded With New Material

KENNETH E. HAGIN

Unless otherwise indicated, all Scripture quotations are taken from the *King James Version* of the Bible.

Scripture quotations marked AMPLIFIED are from *The Amplified Bible*, Old Testament copyright © 1965, 1987 by the Zondervan Corporation. The Amplified New Testament copyright © 1958, 1987 by The Lockman Foundation. Used by permission.

22 21 20 19 18 17 16   17 16 15 14 13 12 11

How You Can Be Led by the Spirit of God
Legacy Edition (paperback)
ISBN-13: 978-0-89276-541-6
ISBN-10: 0-89276-541-0
(formerly ISBN-13: 978-0-89276-535-5 / 10: 0-89276-535-6)

Copyright © 1978, 1989, 2006 Rhema Bible Church
AKA Kenneth Hagin Ministries, Inc.
All rights reserved.
First edition 1978. Second edition 1989.
Legacy edition (clothbound) 2006
Printed in USA

In the U.S. write:
Kenneth Hagin Ministries
P.O. Box 50126
Tulsa, OK 74150-0126
1-888-28-FAITH
rhema.org

In Canada write:
Kenneth Hagin Ministries of Canada
P.O. Box 335, Station D
Etobicoke (Toronto), Ontario
Canada M9A 4X3
1-866-70-RHEMA
rhemacanada.org

If you are born again your conscience is the "Voice" of your (new) spirit (47)

I have the Life of God in me (48) xxx 5:17

Contents

FOREWORD BY KENNETH W. HAGIN vii

PREFACE *Written 50 years of ministry* ix

CHAPTER 1   The Lamp of the Lord 1

CHAPTER 2   Man: An Eternal Spirit 3

CHAPTER 3   Spirit-Conscious 9

CHAPTER 4   What Is the Difference Between Spirit and Soul? 11

CHAPTER 5   The Saving of the Soul 17

CHAPTER 6   Presenting the Body 21

CHAPTER 7   Number One: The Inward Witness 25

CHAPTER 8   Know-So Salvation 33

CHAPTER 9   Fleeced! 35

CHAPTER 10   Following the Witness 39

CHAPTER 11   Number Two: The Inward Voice 43

CHAPTER 12   Effects of the Spirit's Indwelling 47

CHAPTER 13   Two Experiences 53

CHAPTER 14   God Inside 57

CHAPTER 15   Depend on Your Spirit 63

CHAPTER 16   Tenderhearted 67

CHAPTER 17   Feelings: The Voice of the Body 71

CHAPTER 18   Help From Within 77

CHAPTER 19   Number Three: The Voice of the Holy Spirit 81

#1 way to hear (30, 32, 34)

Still small voice (45)

The "Man" (50, 52)

Well (59) Rivers (61) Confess, meditate

65 Kens Healing

(76)

only mountain top

explains (93)

all (3) how we hear

John 16:13 "He will guide you" Rom 8:14,16 "The Spirit Himself bears witness with our spirit" (75)

We perceive – not revelations (101)

(inward witness) Be spirit conscious (only good)

Not the Lord told me

CHAPTER 20 Judging by the Word 85

CHAPTER 21 My Spirit? The Flesh? or the Holy Spirit? 97

CHAPTER 22 I Perceive 101

CHAPTER 23 Spectacular Guidance 103

CHAPTER 24 The Spirit Bade Me Go 107

CHAPTER 25 Guidance Through Prophecy...................................... 111

CHAPTER 26 Guidance Through Visions 121

CHAPTER 27 Listen to Your Heart 131

CHAPTER 28 How to Train the Human Spirit 135

CHAPTER 29 Praying in the Spirit 149

APPENDIXES TO THE LEGACY EDITION

1 Characteristics of a Spirit-Filled Life 151

2 Being Led by the Spirit of God in Prayer 165

3 Being Led by the Holy Spirit in Ministry 181

We perceive

135 (4) Best Meditate again again

Yes Daily (many time)

I AM a spirit being! → Your mind Gets Quiet

*99

I knew your mind will Thinketh my spirit & the (G) will control the body (98)

Your mind will side agree with my spirit & the (G) will control the body (99)

(Divine Nature) Read AK 99

You'll have a body in your heart way spiritual

given Holy Spirit to Help use 164 in hard place 151 psalm

Pray through. 172/79 163

My inward man has the Holy Spirit in His fullness & making His Home in me!

My new spirit has the Life & Nature of God in it! and the Holy Spirit is in it & my spirit is in fellowship with God!

(p98) in it (p98)

Handwritten annotations at top:
Rather than fasting daily, just keep your flesh under All the time. Don't ever let all your flesh wants— (138)

("We having the same Spirit of Faith") 2 Cor 4:13

Foreword
by Kenneth W. Hagin

Handwritten: Faith is in the Spirit, not flesh

For as many as are led by the Spirit of God, they are the sons of God.

—Romans 8:14

Handwritten: 15:4 Faith is the Victory overcomes the world (150)

Today's world is pretty hectic, filled with sounds and images and lots of noise. And all this noise is fighting for our attention and trying to get our focus off of God. Sometimes it's hard to stay focused on God and follow His voice . . . or is it? *Handwritten: Get in the Spirit! Get out of flesh*

We need to remember that as Christians we have a tremendous weapon at our disposal. We have a Friend and Helper living in us—One Who leads and guides us and shows us things to come. He is the mighty Holy Spirit of God, and His job in our lives is to lead us into a victorious life that glorifies God.

One of the main subjects that my father loved to teach on was the Holy Spirit. This book you are holding is some of Dad's finest teaching on the Holy Spirit. Since we released it in 1978, it has gone around the world, been translated into many languages, and changed countless lives. It has opened the eyes of so many to the reality of the Holy Spirit and the truth that God *will* lead us and help us.

As I traveled and worked with Dad over the years, I saw with my own eyes the benefits of being led by the Spirit. Kenneth Hagin Ministries, RHEMA Bible Training Center, and Faith Library Publications would not exist today if a man from McKinney, Texas, had not obeyed the inward leading of the Holy Spirit. His obedience allowed God to bless our family,

Handwritten at bottom: "The spirit of man is the candle of the LORD." We need to be more spirit conscience. PROV 20:27 (135)

vii

this ministry, and countless lives around the world. And if you will learn to follow the Holy Spirit, He will do the same for you!

This Legacy Edition is a tribute to the life and ministry of my dad. By following God, he was able to do so much. And it's a tribute to you—to your hunger and desire to draw closer to God. As you read this classic book and the special added content, draw from the teaching and let it change your heart and life. Choose to follow Him and don't rely on your own strength. Let the Holy Spirit guide you and see all that God can do in you and through you!

In His Love,

Kenneth W. Hagin

Kenneth W. Hagin

When they're a gift it praize

prayer

Prayer must = praise to receive (p.160)

(p.160) Answers to All prayers!

Preface

In February 1959 in El Paso, Texas, the Lord appeared to me in a vision. He came into my room at 6:30 in the evening, sat down in a chair by my bedside, and talked with me for an hour and a half. I tell more about this in the book, but I want to emphasize something here first.

He talked to me about the ministry of the prophet (Eph. 4:11–12). Then He said, "I did not put prophets in the Church to guide the New Testament Church. My Word says, 'As many as are led by the Spirit of God, they are the sons of God' (Rom. 8:14). Now if you will listen to Me, I am going to teach you how to follow My Spirit. Then I want you to teach My people how to be led by the Spirit."

I am ashamed that I have let many years go by without teaching too much along this line. Occasionally, I would get into the edge of it, but I did not really *teach* on it.

So in recent times, the Lord has stirred me up and now I am beginning to teach more on this subject. This book is part of that stirring.

Kenneth E. Hagin

CHAPTER 1

The Lamp of the Lord

For as many as are led by the Spirit of God,
they are the sons of God.

—Romans 8:14

The Spirit itself [Himself] *beareth witness with our spirit,*
that we are the children of God.

—Romans 8:16

The spirit of man is the candle of the Lord, searching
all the inward parts of the belly.

—Proverbs 20:27

Children of God can expect to be led by the Spirit of God.

Another translation of Proverbs 20:27 reads, "The spirit of man
is the *lamp* of the Lord . . ." Had this verse been written today it

might have read, "The spirit of man is the *light bulb* of the Lord." What it means is this: _God will enlighten us—He will guide us—through our spirits._

Many times, however, we seek guidance by means other than the way God said. When we do, we get into trouble. We sometimes judge how God is leading by what our physical senses tell us. But nowhere does God say that God will guide us through our physical senses. Too often we look at things from a mental standpoint and endeavor to reason out things. But nowhere does the Bible say God will guide us through our mentality. The Bible does not say that the body of man is the candle of the Lord, nor that the mind of man is the candle of the Lord. It says that the spirit of man is the candle of the Lord (Prov. 20:27).

God will guide us—He will enlighten us—through our spirits.

Now before we can understand how God does lead us and guide us through our spirits, we have to understand the nature of man. We have to understand that man is a spirit, that he has a soul, and that he lives in a body.

CHAPTER 2

Man: An Eternal Spirit

And God said, Let us make man in our image,
after our likeness: . . .
So God created man in his own image,
in the image of God created he him . . . .

—Genesis 1:26–27

Man is a spirit being. He is made in the likeness of God. Jesus said that God is a Spirit (John 4:24). So man must of necessity be a spirit.

Man is a spirit, he has a soul, and he lives in a physical body (1 Thess. 5:23).

When the physical body of man is dead and in the grave, the spirit lives on. That part of man is eternal. Spirits can never die, and man is a spirit. Paul is speaking of physical death here:

PHILIPPIANS 1:23–24

23 For I am in a strait betwixt two, having a desire to depart, and to be with Christ; which is far better:

24 Nevertheless to abide in the flesh is more needful for you.

Paul is going to live. Whether in the body or out of the body, he is still going to live. If he abides, or lives in the flesh he can teach the church at Philippi and be a blessing to them. That would be more needful for them. It would be far better for Paul himself, however, to depart and be with Christ. Paul was actually saying, "I am going to live in the body or I am going to depart and be with Christ."

Who is going to depart?

"*I*" am going to depart. Paul was not talking about his body. His body was not going to depart. Paul is talking about the inward man, the spirit man, who lives inside the body.

People sometimes ask, "Will we know one another in Heaven?"

I always quickly ask, "Do you know one another down here?"

You see, *you* are the one who is going to be there. If *you* know one another down here, *you* will know one another there. *You* are the one who is here, and *you* will be the one who is there.

"*I* am going to depart," Paul says, "and be with Christ which is *far better.*" I like that! If he had just said it was better, that would have been good. But he said, "It is *far better!*"

Some false cults teach that when a man dies he is dead like a dog is dead when it dies. No, man is not. Man is more than a body. He is a spirit, he has a soul, and he lives in a body. Others say that when man dies he is in "soul sleep." The Bible does not teach that. Some say the spirit does depart all right—but it comes back as a cow, a dog, or as someone else. Reincarnation is unscriptural and unbiblical. Stay with the Word of God and it will solve all your problems along this line. Paul said, "*I* am going to depart. I am going to be with the Lord, which is *far better.*"

Paul preached the same truths and taught the same facts to all the churches. Here he uses different words to teach the same blessed truth to the church at Corinth:

2 CORINTHIANS 4:16

16 . . . but though our outward man perish, yet the inward man is renewed day by day.

There is an *inward* man. And there is an *outward* man. The outward man is not the real you. The outward man is only the house in which you live. The inward man is the real you. The inward man never grows older. He is renewed day by day. The inward man is a spirit man.

What is our spirit? Keep in mind our introductory texts. Romans 8:14 says, "*. . . as many as are led by the Spirit of God, they are the sons of God.*" Then verse 16 gives us a little insight into how the Spirit of God leads us: "*The Spirit itself* [Himself] *beareth witness with our spirit, that we are the children of God.*" In other words, the Spirit of God bears witness with the spirit of man. Proverbs 20:27 says, "*The spirit of man is the candle of the Lord. . . .*" According to these scriptures God will guide us through our spirits; therefore, we must find out what our spirit is.

Jesus said to Nicodemus, "*. . . except a man be born again, he cannot see the kingdom of God*" (John 3:3).

Nicodemus, being natural, could only think naturally. So he said, "*. . . How can a man be born when he is old? can he enter the second time into his mother's womb, and be born?*" (v. 4).

Jesus was not talking about a physical birth. He said, *"That which is born of the flesh is flesh and that which is born of the Spirit is spirit"* (v. 6). He was talking about a *spiritual* birth.

The part of man that is born again is his spirit. Man's spirit receives *eternal life*—the life of God, and the nature of God. It is man's spirit that is made a new creature in Christ.

Paul calls man's spirit "the inward man." Peter calls man's spirit "the hidden man of the heart."

1 PETER 3:4

4 But let it be the hidden man of the heart, in that which is not corruptible, even the ornament of a meek and quiet spirit, which is in the sight of God of great price.

In many places when the Bible speaks of the heart, it is speaking of the spirit. This is the real man. It will help you in your believing and in your faith to think like that. In the New Testament, wherever the word *heart* is used, substitute the word *spirit* and you will get a clearer picture of what the Bible is talking about. It is the spirit of man that is born again.

2 CORINTHIANS 5:17

17 Therefore if any man be in Christ, he is a new creature: old things are passed away; behold, all things are become new.

This is talking about the inward man. It couldn't be talking about the outward man. When you are born again and become a new creature, you do not get a new body. The outward man is just like it was before. If you were bald before you were born again, you are still bald afterwards. If you had brown eyes before, you still have brown eyes. The outward man does not change. God does not do anything with the outward man. (You have to do something with the outward man. You find out what God wants you to do with the outward man from the Bible—and then *you* do it.) God does something with the inward man. He makes the man on the inside a new man in Christ, a new creature—a new creation.

CHAPTER 3

Spirit-Conscious

. . . I pray God your whole spirit and soul and
body be preserved blameless.

—1 Thessalonians 5:23

In this scriptural passage, Paul begins with the inside, the innermost part of man, the heart of his being, which is his spirit, and comes to the outside.

Yet most people misquote this verse. They say, "body, soul, and spirit." Why do they put the body first? Because they are more body-conscious than spirit-conscious. Natural things mean more to them than spiritual things. So they put physical things first.

Sometimes we are more mental-conscious because we live more in the mental realm.

But man is a spirit being. We need to be spirit-conscious. Spiritual things will become more real to us the more spirit-conscious we become.

If we are going to be led by the Spirit of God, we must become more spirit-conscious, or we'll miss out on the whole thing. God's Spirit leads us through our spirits.

Put spirit first. Become more spirit-conscious, more conscious of the inward man. Realize that you are a spirit being and that you became a new creation re-created by God in Christ Jesus. It will help you grow—*spiritually*.

Many years ago I began to think like this, and at first I would say it to myself out loud: *I am a spirit being. I have a soul. And I live in a body.*

Saying that helped me become more spirit-conscious. It helped my faith, because faith is of the spirit, or the heart.

CHAPTER 4

What Is the Difference Between Spirit and Soul?

For the word of God is quick, and powerful, and sharper
than any two-edged sword, piercing even to the
dividing asunder of soul and spirit. . . .

—Hebrews 4:12

The spirit and the soul are not the same.

Many years ago, back in the early '50s, I began an intensive study on this subject. I got books from the leading Bible schools and seminaries, both Pentecostal and denominational, to see what they taught on the subject of man. None satisfied me. None were actually scriptural. They were only scriptural, as the Bible says, "in part." I asked leading Bible scholars and ministers across the nation. You would recognize some of their names if I mentioned them. I even heard someone ask one of today's most well-known ministers, "What is the difference between the spirit and the soul?" He looked startled and said, "I thought they were the same." That was the answer I got from most of the ministers I asked.

Yet how could they be the same? Paul, by the Spirit of God, said they can be divided by the Word of God (Heb. 4:12). If you can divide them, they cannot be the same.

Only the Word of God can divide the spirit and the soul, however. The reason we have not been able to distinguish between them is that we have not dug deeply enough into the Word. Years ago, in the western part of the United States, they had what we call "the gold rush." People rushed out West. They were going to get rich in a hurry. Most panned a little gold out of creeks. Some found a few nuggets lying on the ground. But if you really wanted to strike it rich, you had to dig for it. The same is true in spiritual matters: You can skim along on the surface of the Bible and pan out a little gold here and there—and even find a nugget occasionally. But if you really want to strike it rich, you have to dig down deep into the Word of God.

For 15 years I studied carefully, burning the midnight oil. If there was anything I desired to know it was the difference between the spirit and the soul. Eventually, I went through this process of elimination. I wrote it down like this: *With my body I contact the physical realm.* (That goes without argument.) *With my spirit I contact the spiritual realm.* That left only one other part of me that made contact with any other realm. I knew then that it had to be with my soul that I contacted the intellectual or soulish realm (which includes the emotions and the intellect). So I wrote: *With my soul I contact the intellectual realm.* Here is a scripture that helped me:

1 CORINTHIANS 14:14

14 For if I pray in an unknown tongue, my spirit prayeth, but my understanding is unfruitful.

The Amplified translation reads, "For if I pray in an [unknown] tongue, my spirit [by the Holy Spirit within me] prays, but my mind is unproductive. . . ."

Our understanding, our natural human mentality, is a part of our soul.

Notice what Paul said. "My spirit prays, but my understanding is unfruitful." He did not say, "When I pray in an unknown tongue my soul prays." He did not say, "When I pray in tongues, I pray out of my intellect, or out of my mind." He said in effect, "I am not praying out of my soul when I pray in tongues; I am praying out of my spirit, my heart, my innermost being." Do you remember what Jesus said?

JOHN 7:37–39

37 In the last day, that great day of the feast, Jesus stood and cried, saying, If any man thirst, let him come unto me, and drink.

38 He that believeth on me, as the scripture hath said, OUT OF HIS BELLY shall flow rivers of living water.

39 (BUT THIS SPAKE HE OF THE SPIRIT, which they that believe on him should receive: for the Holy Ghost was not yet given; because that Jesus was not yet glorified.)

As a result of receiving the Holy Spirit, Jesus said, "out of the belly shall flow rivers of living water." Another translation reads, "out of the innermost being will flow rivers of living water."

A Full Gospel pastor's daughter was six years old when she and some of the children were off by themselves one night at a revival. Some of these youngsters were filled with the Holy Spirit and began to speak with other tongues. This little six-year-old, holding her stomach, ran up to her mother, saying, "Momma, Momma, that came right out of my belly."

She was being scriptural. She was speaking in tongues from her belly—her spirit, her innermost being. That's where tongues come from—the Holy Spirit who resides in your spirit gives your spirit the utterance and you speak it out.

Consider these scriptures together now. *"The spirit of man is the candle of the Lord, searching all the INWARD PARTS OF THE BELLY . . . OUT OF HIS BELLY shall flow rivers of living water. . . ."*

All the leadings I have ever received have come from out of my spirit. And most of them have come while I was praying in other tongues. You can understand why. Your spirit is active when you are praying in tongues.

One reason the church world as a whole has failed so miserably is that it has done so much of just one kind of praying—praying with the understanding, or *mental* praying. Christians have endeavored to fight spiritual battles with mental abilities.

I have learned this through these many, many years. In every crisis of life I have learned to look to my spirit inside me. I have learned to pray in other tongues. While I am praying in other tongues, guidance comes up from inside me. This is because my spirit is active. My body is not active, my mind (my soul) is not active, but my spirit is active, and it is through my spirit that God is going to guide me.

Sometimes I interpret what I am praying in tongues, and through the interpretation I receive light and guidance (1 Cor. 14:13). But most of the time, that is not so. Most of the time, just while I am praying in tongues, from somewhere way down inside, I can sense something rise up in me. It begins to take shape and form. I cannot tell anyone mentally how I know it, because my understanding has nothing to do with it. But I know on the inside of me what to do.

I follow that. I listen to my spirit. Because the spirit of man is the candle of the Lord.

CHAPTER 5

The Saving of the Soul

. . . receive with meekness the engrafted word,
which is able to save your souls.

—James 1:21

T he spirit of man is the part of man that is born again. It is the
part of man that receives *eternal life*, which is the nature and life
of God. It is the spirit of man that becomes a new creature in Christ
Jesus. The soul is not the innermost being at all. It is not the soul that
is born again. The saving of the soul is a process.

James 1:21 used to bother me when I was a denominational
preacher before I was filled with the Holy Spirit. I didn't know what
I know now. I used spirit and soul interchangeably—referring to the
spirit as the soul, and the soul as the spirit. I didn't divide them as the
Bible does. But I did have enough sense to leave this verse alone until
I grew so that I could understand what it is saying.

The Epistle of James was not written to sinners. James did not write a letter to the world; he wrote this letter to the Church. We know that because of James chapter 5 where he says, *"Is any sick among you? let him call for the elders of the church . . ."* (v. 14). In other words, if there is any sick among the Church, let him call for the elders of the Church. Also referring back to the first chapter of James, let's pick up with verse 18:

JAMES 1:18–21

18 Of his own will begat he us with the word of truth, that we should be a kind of firstfruits of his creatures.

19 Wherefore, my beloved brethren, let every man be swift to hear, slow to speak, slow to wrath:

20 For the wrath of man worketh not the righteousness of God.

21 Wherefore lay apart all filthiness and superfluity of naughtiness, and receive with meekness the engrafted word, which is able to save your souls.

James is talking to born-again believers. Of the Father's own will, he writes, we were begotten, or born again by the Word of Truth. He calls them "my beloved brethren," so they were in Christ. Yet he encourages these born-again, Spirit-filled people to receive the engrafted Word with meekness, *". . . which is able to save your souls."* Evidently, their souls were not saved.

You see, a man's spirit, the innermost man, the real man, receives eternal life and is born again. But his intellect and emotions—which comprise his soul—still have to be dealt with. They are not born again. They are to be renewed.

Paul speaks about the renewing of the mind, writing to the saints at Rome.

ROMANS 12:2

2 And be not conformed to this world: but be ye transformed by the renewing of your mind, that ye may prove what is that good, and acceptable, and perfect, will of God.

The Psalmist David spoke of the restoring of the soul:

PSALM 23:3

3 He restoreth my soul . . .

The Hebrew word translated *restore* in the Old Testament, and the Greek word translated *renew* in the New Testament mean about the same thing. The soul—the mind—is to be renewed or restored.

My mother left me a chair that she inherited from her mother. I don't know exactly how old that chair is, but it is quite old. I can remember when my grandmother had it restored. They put new upholstery on it. They revarnished it. It was still the same chair; it was just restored. It was renewed.

In the Word it is never written that God restores our spirits. Our spirits become brand-new creatures in Christ Jesus. Our souls, however, must be renewed or restored.

How? We have these scriptures relative to the soul:

"*. . . receive with meekness the engrafted word, which is able to save your souls . . . be not conformed to this world but be ye transformed by the renewing of your mind, that ye may prove what is that good, and acceptable, and perfects, will of God . . . He restoreth my soul*" (James 1:21; Rom. 12:2; Ps. 23:3).

Man's soul is saved, or restored, when his mind becomes renewed with the Word of God. It is the Word of God that saves our souls, that renews our minds, that restores our souls.

When our minds become renewed with the Word of God, then we think in line with what God's Word says. We are able to know and prove the permissive and the perfect will of God—because the Word of God is the will of God. We don't have so many questions about the will of God once we get our souls saved.

The greatest need in the Church today is to have minds renewed with the Word of God.

CHAPTER *6*

Presenting the Body

I beseech you therefore, brethren, by the mercies of God,
that ye present your bodies a living sacrifice, holy, acceptable unto God,
which is your reasonable service.

—Romans 12:1

It is the inward man—not the outward man—that becomes a new creature in Christ. We still have the same body we had before we became a new creature. What we must learn to do is to let that new man on the inside of us dominate. With that new man, we control the flesh and do something with our bodies.

Let's look again at Second Corinthians 5:17 which says, *"Therefore if any man be in Christ, he is a new creature: old things are passed away; behold, all things are become new."* One translation reads, "If any man be in Christ, there is a new self...."

Sometimes in churches we hear people talk about "dying out to self." There is no such statement in the Bible. We don't need to die out to self if we have become a new self. What we need to do is crucify the flesh. The Bible does talk about that.

Crucifying the flesh is not something God does for you. it is something you do for yourself. *"I beseech you therefore, brethren,"* Paul wrote to the Church, *"by the mercies of God, that ye present your bodies . . ."* (Rom. 12:1).

Who presents your body?

You do.

Who is *you*?

That's the man on the inside who is born again, and has become a new creature.

You do something with your body. If *you* do not do something with it, nothing will ever be done with it.

1 CORINTHIANS 9:27

27 But I keep under my body, and bring it into subjection: lest that by any means, when I have preached to others, I myself should be a castaway [disapproved].

Here Paul is talking about the fact that *he* does something with his body. *"I keep under my body. I bring it into subjection."*

Who is *I*?

That's the real man—the real Paul—the man on the inside who has become a new creature in Christ Jesus and is filled with the Holy Spirit. *"I do something with my body. I keep it under. I bring it into subjection."*

What did Paul bring his body into subjection to?

To the inward man. Instead of letting the body dominate the inward man, Paul saw to it that the inward man dominated the outward man.

Now notice this. Here is this great apostle, this holy man of God, this man who wrote half the New Testament, a man who is a spiritual giant—yet evidently his body wanted to do things that were wrong. If it hadn't, he would not have had to keep it under. He would not have had to bring it into subjection.

Just because your body wants to do wrong, doesn't mean you are not saved, or that you are not filled with the Holy Spirit. (If that were the case, Paul was not saved.) You will have to contend with the body, the flesh, as long as you are in this world.

"Brother Hagin, I want you to pray for me," one man said.

"What for?" I asked. I like to know what I am praying for.

A look of seriousness, even tears, came to his eyes, "I want you to pray that I will never have any more trouble with the devil."

I said, "Do you want me to pray you will die?"

"No, no, I don't want to die."

I said, "The only way you won't have any more trouble with the devil is to get out of here and go on to Heaven."

You will have problems with the devil as long as you are in this life. You will have problems with the flesh as long as you are in the flesh. But, blessed be God, the means, the ability, and the authority have been given to you through the Word of God to deal with the devil and to deal with the flesh.

Paul did not let his body dominate him. The man on the inside— the man Who was born again and filled with the Holy Spirit—must dominate the outward man.

You can do it. What I want you to see is this—*you* are the one who *must* do it. Paul did not say God would do it for you. He did not say the Holy Spirit would do it for you. He said, "*You* present your bodies." He said, "*You* be not conformed to this world." He said, "*You* be transformed by the renewing of your mind." *You* present your body. *You* do it. *You* get your mind renewed with the Word of God. *You* do it.

The life and nature of God is inside your spirit. Let that man on the inside be the dominant one. Listen to him. It is the spirit of man that is the candle of the Lord. It is through your spirit that God will guide you.

CHAPTER 7

Number One:
The Inward Witness

The Spirit itself [Himself] *beareth*
witness with our spirit. . . .

—Romans 8:16

Y ou will find that being led by the inward witness is the
number one way, or the primary way, that God leads all of
His children.

Let me go back—I said I would in the preface of this book—to
what Jesus said to me in February 1959 in El Paso, Texas. It was 6:30
in the evening. I was sitting up in bed studying. My eyes were wide
open. (There are three types of visions. The highest type is an open
vision. In an open vision, one's physical senses are not suspended,

and his physical eyes are not closed. He possesses all of his physical capabilities, yet sees into the realm of the spirit.)

I heard footsteps. The door to my room was ajar 12 to 14 inches, so I looked to see who was coming into my room. I expected to see some literal, physical person. But as I looked to see who it was, I saw Jesus. It seemed as if the hair on my neck and head stood straight up on end. Chill bumps popped out all over my body.

I saw Him. He had on a white robe. He wore Roman sandals. (Jesus has appeared to me eight times. Every time, except this time, His feet were bare. This time He had on sandals; that's what I had heard as He approached my door.) He seemed to be about 5 feet 11 inches tall. He looked as if He weighed about 180 pounds.

He came through the door and pushed it back until it was almost shut. He walked around the foot of my bed. I followed Him with my eyes—almost spellbound. He took a hold of a straight chair and pushed it up close to my bed. Then He sat down on it, folded His hands, and began His conversation with me by saying, "I told you in the automobile the other night. . . ."

The automobile had been full. My wife and I and others were driving along within two blocks of where I now was, as Jesus sat by my bedside talking to me. In the car, I had heard the Spirit of God speak to me. I thought everyone in the car had heard it and I said, "Did you all hear that?" They said, "No, we didn't hear anything."

In the Old Testament the prophets would say, "And the Word of the Lord came unto me saying. . . ." Did you ever wonder how it came? It could not have been literally audible. If it had been audible everyone present would have heard it—the prophet would not have had to tell the people what the Spirit said. The Word of the Lord came to the prophet's spirit from the Spirit of God. It is so real that it seems audible at the time. The Word of the Lord was so real to me, I thought everyone in the car had heard it too.

As Jesus sat at my bedside, He said, "I spoke to you the night before last in the automobile and told you certain things. I told you, by my Spirit, that later I would talk to you further. So now I have come to talk to you about this. . . ."

It was concerning the ministry of the prophet. Jesus sat there in that chair and talked to me for an hour and a half. And I talked to Him. I asked questions in reference to what He was saying. He answered them. I will not go into all He said about the prophet's ministry that is another message. But I will get into some of it.

Jesus said to me, "The prophet of the New Testament is very similar to the prophet of the Old Testament in that the prophet of the Old Testament was called a 'seer' because he saw and knew things supernaturally. The prophet of the New Testament also sees and knows things supernaturally. But the prophet of the New Testament does not have the same status as the prophet of the Old Testament, in that I did not set prophets in the Church to guide the Church. A Christian under the New Testament need not seek guidance through prophets. He might receive guidance through prophets, but he should not seek it. It is unscriptural to do so. The ministry of the New Testament prophet in this area is only to confirm what people already have in their own spirits.

"Under the Old Covenant, only the priest, the prophet, and the king were anointed by the Holy Spirit to stand in those offices. What you would call the laity did not have the Spirit of God upon them or in them. Therefore, under the Old Covenant, people would seek guidance through the prophet because he had the Spirit of God."

Under the New Testament, thanks be to God, we not only have the Spirit of God *upon* us—we have Him in us!

Jesus also said to me, "Under the New Covenant, it does not say, 'As many as are led by prophets, they are the sons of God.' The New

Testament says, *'For as many as are led by the Spirit of God, they are the sons of God'*" (Rom. 8:14).

Then He said, "The number one way, the primary way, that I lead all of My children is by the inward witness. I am going to show you how that works so you won't make the mistakes you have made in the past."

Jesus explained to me that to stand in the office of the prophet, one is first of all a minister of the Gospel separated and called to the ministry with the call of God upon his life. Secondly, he has at least two of the revelation gifts—the word of wisdom, the word of knowledge, the discerning of spirits—plus the gift of prophecy, operating in his ministry.

Then He called my attention to something that had been happening to me for the previous three days. For the past three days, I had sat down to write a letter to a pastor confirming a date to hold a meeting for him. Somehow, the first day, I got about half a page written, then I tore it up and threw it into the wastebasket. The next day I did the same thing. The third day I did the same thing. Then it was the day that the Lord was here in the room talking to me.

Jesus said, "You see Me sitting here talking to you. This is a manifestation of the Spirit called discerning of spirits. (Discerning of spirits is seeing into the spirit realm.) This is the prophet's ministry in operation. You are seeing into the realm of the spirit. You see Me. You hear Me talking. I am bringing you, through the vision, a word of knowledge and also a word of wisdom. I am telling you not to go to that church. The pastor would not accept the way you would minister when you got there. But I am never going to lead you this way again. (He never has, and that was many years ago.) From now on, I'm going to lead you by the inward witness. You had the inward witness all the time. You had a check in your spirit. That's the reason you tore up the letter three times. You had something on the inside, *a check, a red light, a stop signal.* It wasn't even a voice that said, *'Don't go.'* It was just an *inward intuition.*"

Then Jesus reminded me of another invitation. I had preached a convention for one of the Full Gospel denominations the previous year. Nearly every pastor there asked me if I would come and hold a meeting. I had hundreds of calls, I suppose.

One fellow came up to me and said, "Brother Hagin, do you ever go to small churches?"

I said, "I go anywhere the Lord says to go."

"Well, we only run 70 to 90 in Sunday school. But if God ever speaks to you, we want you to come."

I dismissed that conversation along with many others. Several months later, however, while praying in the church one day about my services that night, that conversation came back to me. Then every day it continued to come back to me. Finally, after about 30 or 40 days, I said, "Lord, do You want me to go to that little church for a meeting?"

The more I would pray about it and the more I would think about it, as we say, the better I would feel about it on the inside of me. It wasn't a physical feeling, but it was a feeling in my spirit.

Sitting by my bedside, Jesus referred to this: "The more you thought about it, the better you felt about it. You had a *velvety-like* feeling in your spirit. That's the *green light.* That's the *go-ahead signal.* That's the *witness of the Spirit* to go! Now you see Me sitting here, you hear Me talking to you, and I am telling you to go to that church. But I am never going to lead you to go anywhere like this again. (He never has.) From now on, I am going to lead you just like I do every other Christian—by the inward witness."

Then the Lord said this to me, which is not just for my benefit, but also for yours: "If you will learn to follow that inward witness, I will make you rich. I will guide you in all the affairs of life, financial as well as spiritual. [Some think God is only interested in their spiritual well being, and nothing else. But He is interested in everything we are interested in.] I am not opposed to My children being rich; I am opposed to their being covetous."

I have followed that inward witness and He has done just what He said He would do. He has made me rich.

Someone asked, "Are you a millionaire?"

I didn't say that. Some people fail to realize what the word "rich" means. It means a full supply. It means abundant provision. I have more than a full supply. I have more than an abundant provision. It is because I learned to follow the leading of the Spirit by the inward witness.

What He did for me, He will do for you. It won't come overnight, or by next Saturday night. But as you learn to develop your spirit and follow that inward witness, He will guide you in every area of your life.

I knew a man down in Texas. He had never worn a pair of shoes until he was 12 years old. He only had a fifth grade education. But way back when money was money, he was a millionaire.

Two different people, one from California and the other from Minnesota who had been frequent house guests in his home, told me that this man told each of them the same thing.

He said to them both, "In all these years and in all these investments [that's how he made his money], I have never lost a dime."

That beats my record. How about yours?

"Everything I have ever invested in, has made money," he told each of them on different occasions. Then he told them how he did it.

"I always do this. When someone comes along with an idea, wanting me to invest in something, my first reaction is mental. Now I know when Jesus said, 'When you pray, enter into your closet,' that He didn't necessarily mean you have to get into a closet to pray. I know He meant for us to shut things out. But I have a large closet in my bedroom where I go to pray. I pray about it. I wait long enough—until I hear what my spirit says. Sometimes I wait three days. Now I don't mean that I stay in there 24 hours a day. I might come out and eat one meal. Usually I miss a few. I come out and sleep a little bit. But the majority of the time I am waiting, just by myself, until I know inside by an inward witness what I am to do.

"Sometimes my head says, 'Boy, you would be a fool to put your money in that. You'll lose your shirt.' But my heart says, 'Go ahead and invest in it.' So I do. And in all these years, I have never lost a dime.

"Then again, someone comes along with a deal and my head says, 'Boy, you had better get in on that one.' But I don't pay any attention to my head. I get in that closet and wait. Sometimes all night long I wait. I'll pray and read my Bible, but a lot of the time I just wait. I just get quiet until I can hear inside what my heart says. When my heart says, 'No, don't do it,' and my head says, 'Yes, you'd better get in on it,' I don't do it."

What had this man done? He had learned to follow the inward witness and God had guided him in his business, until in the late '30s and the early '40s he was already worth two million dollars. That doesn't sound big now, but it was big then.

Do you think God loved him more than He loves you? No, but this man took time to listen to God. *He took steps and means and measures to wait upon God.*

I was with a group of ministers and we were talking personally, and conversing with one another. Someone asked a certain individual who is a very successful minister, "Now we know that God called you and that the anointing of God's Spirit is upon you. But from your standpoint, is there any *one* thing you do that you would say has contributed more to your success than any other one thing?"

That man said, "I always follow my deepest premonitions."

What was he saying? He was simply saying, "I always listen to my spirit. I do what my spirit tells me to do. I follow that inward witness."

The inward witness is just as supernatural as guidance through visions and so on; it is just not as spectacular. Many people are looking for the spectacular and missing the supernatural that is right there all the time.

CHAPTER *8*

Know-So Salvation

*He that believeth on the Son of God hath
the witness in himself. . . .*

—1 John 5:10

"*For as many as are led by the Spirit of God, they are the sons of God*" (Rom. 8:14). The sons of God can expect to be led by the Spirit of God. Hallelujah! They are not led by someone else telling them what to do. The Holy Spirit is going to lead us. We have Scripture that says so.

How does He lead? Verse 16 gives us a clue: "*The Spirit itself* [Himself] *BEARETH WITNESS with our spirit, that we are the children of God*" (Rom. 8:16).

In the most important aspect of life, and in the most important thing that can happen to you—becoming a child of God—God lets

Ron

you know that you are His child by His Spirit *bearing witness* with your spirit. Then you can understand that the first and foremost way God will *lead* you is also by that inward witness.

You do not know that you are a child of God because someone prophesied that you are. You wouldn't accept that. You do not know that you are a child of God because someone said, "I *feel* like you are." You wouldn't accept that. You are not a child of God because you had a vision. You might, or you might not have had a vision, but a vision is not what would make you a child of God. That is not what the Bible says. That is not the way you know you are a child of God.

How does the Bible say we know we are children of God? *His Spirit, God's Spirit, bears witness with our spirits.*

Sometimes you can't really explain how you know you are a child of God, but you just know it, right down on the inside of you. You know it! You know you are by the inward witness.

I was born again as a teenager on the bed of sickness April 22, 1933. Since that day, the thought has never occurred to me that I might not be saved. Yet even as a young Christian I ran into people who said, "You're not saved because you don't belong to *our* church." Or those who would argue, "You're not saved because you haven't been baptized *our* way." And many gave me other reasons why they thought I was not saved.

But none of that disturbed me. I laughed at it, *because I had the witness! And I had the love!*

1 JOHN 3:14

14 We know that we have passed from death unto life, because we love. . . .

CHAPTER *9*

Fleeced!

A new heart also will I give you, and a new spirit will I put within you:
and I will take away the stony heart out of your flesh, and I will give you
an heart of flesh. And I will put my spirit within you. . . .

—Ezekiel 36:26–27

In 1941 I didn't know as much as I know now. Please don't misunderstand me; I don't know as much now as I am going to know. I would hate to think I know all I am ever going to know in this life about God and about the Bible. No, we don't know everything, but praise God for what we do know.

Anyway, in 1941 my wife and I were pastors of a church in the blackland of North Central Texas. Another church down in the oil field of East Texas wanted me to come and try out as pastor. So I drove down and preached one Sunday. The church asked if they could vote on me for pastor, and I said yes. Traveling back home after the service, I put out a fleece.

Now I was born and raised Southern Baptist. I started preaching as a Southern Baptist. In 1937 I was baptized in the Holy Spirit as a Baptist preacher. In 1939 I accepted the pastorate of a little Full Gospel Church. It was in March 1941 that this church in East Texas wanted to consider me as pastor. I had been with Full Gospel people long enough by that time that some of their misconceptions had rubbed off on me. Don't misunderstand me; a lot of good things rubbed off on me too. But this one was bad. I kept hearing them talk about putting out fleeces. So I put out a fleece.

I really knew better. But at the time it seemed as if it would save me a lot of the trouble of praying, and getting alone and waiting on God, and maybe some fasting—just to put out a fleece.

In putting out a fleece, one prays something like this: "Lord, if you want me to do this—then You do that." Or, "God, if you want me to do this, then have that happen." Or, "Lord, shut that door, and open this door." *Show me like Gideon!*

Some of those doors the devil might shut, and some of them the devil might open. They are in his territory. The Bible calls him the god of this world (2 Cor. 4:4). That would be like praying, "Lord, if you want me to go to Kansas City next week, You open Brother Hagin's front door." I might open it myself. I live there. You see, Satan can move in the sense realm.

God has a better way of leading His children than by a hit-and-miss method such as fleeces. The New Testament does not say, "As many as are led by fleeces, they are the children of God."

"Yes," someone might say, "but Gideon put out a fleece back in the Old Testament."

Why go back under the Old Covenant? We have something better. The Old Covenant is for spiritually dead people. I am not spiritually dead. I am alive! I have the Spirit of God in me.

Remember Gideon was not a prophet, a priest, or a king. Only those three offices, under the Old Covenant, were anointed by the Spirit of God. The Spirit of God was not personally present with the rest of the people.

That's why every male had to present himself at the temple in Jerusalem once a year. The Shekinah glory—the Presence of God—was kept shut up in the Holy of Holies. But when Jesus died on Calvary, the curtain that curtained off the Holy of Holies was rent (torn) in twain from top to bottom—and God moved out. He has never dwelled in earth-made houses since. He dwells in us!

It is dangerous for New Testament, Spirit-filled Christians to put out fleeces. I know that from the Word. And I know it from experience.

Back there in 1941 I said as I drove along, "Lord, I am going to put out a fleece. I am just going to turn it over to You. (I didn't realize that I wasn't turning it over to the Lord.) If they elect me as pastor 100 percent, I am going to accept that as being the will of God, and I am going to accept that church."

I got every vote! That was my fleece. They elected me 100 percent. They missed God. I missed God. They got fleeced. I got fleeced. I got out of the perfect will of God—and God just let me do it.

We moved into the parsonage. Many things were more comfortable than what we'd had before, from the natural standpoint. We had more money. We lived in a better parsonage. We drove a better automobile.

But I would study and pray and get a message—and be just all on fire. Then the minute I stepped inside the church door, it was as though somebody poured a bucket of cold water on me. I lost it all. In fourteen months I didn't preach a decent sermon. No inspiration.

My wife was reluctant to say anything. She finally did say, "Honey, you've got to where you can make a pretty good talk."

That was all I was doing, making "talks." I wasn't preaching. When my agreed-upon time was up, I left. I didn't wait for some signal to leave; I just left.

Later on in pastoring, I always wanted to go back there for a meeting because I wanted those people to know I could preach. They had never really heard me *preach*. Finally, in the course of time, I went back and held a revival. Folks' mouths fell open. "We didn't know you could preach like that," they said.

I said, "Oh, yes, I preached like that before I came here to pastor, and I preached like that after I left here."

"Well, you didn't preach like that when you were here." I said, "No, because we were all out of the will of God. I was here out of the will of God, and you elected me out of the will of God."

I learned about that fleece business. One time ought to cure a fellow. But some folks—even though none of their fleeces have ever worked—still put out fleeces.

I never missed it again in going to any other church as pastor. And I didn't put out any more fleeces. I prayed and waited on God. I talked to God long enough so that I knew right on the inside what I was to do.

CHAPTER 10

Following the Witness

For thou wilt light my candle:
the Lord my God will enlighten my darkness.

—Psalm 18:28

We left that church. We were asked by leaders of a denomination to take another church to fill in temporarily, so we did.

Later, while I would be in my study praying, I would get a burden to go back to the church I'd left as a result of the fleece. I hadn't finished what God wanted me to do there.

Usually this happened when I was praying about my sermon and the Sunday services in other tongues—because remember, when I pray in tongues, my spirit prays, and the spirit of man is the candle of the Lord. I would get such a burden for the church I had left more years before, I would jump up and run out of the room to from it.

Once I came to myself out in the street beside the church wondering, *How did I get out here?* To get out there I would have had to run out of the church study, across the auditorium, and out the side door. But I didn't remember doing that. I was under such a burden for that church, and I was trying to get away from it. I didn't want to go back there to pastor.

Finally, after about 30 days of that, I said, "Lord, are You talking to me about going back there? Are You trying to give me some guidance?" Then I said, "Talk to my wife. She can listen too."

One morning while we washed dishes, I said to my wife, "Honey, if the Lord says anything to you, let me know." I didn't tell her anything more.

Then I waited 30 days. You don't have to get in a big hurry about some things. The Bible says, ". . . *he that believeth shall not make haste*" (Isa. 28:16). Faith doesn't get in a hurry. The devil will try to push you. He will say, "Hurry up. Hurry up. Hurry, hurry, hurry." He will try to move you out of faith, move you into doubt, move you into unbelief, and get you away from the leading of God.

Thirty days later, as I washed the dishes and my wife dried them, I said, "Has the Lord been talking to you?"

"If He has, I don't know it."

I got a little more pointed in order to bring her out. I said, "Has the Lord said anything to you about going back to _____?" I called the name of the city where the church was.

"Oh," she said, "I thought that was just me."

"Well," I said, "let's analyze what you mean when you say me."

If you mean the flesh, then that wouldn't be right. But if you mean the real "me," the man on the inside—the real you—then that is right.

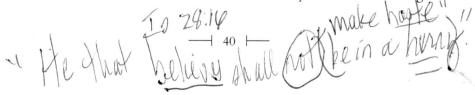

Remember that the spirit is the candle of the Lord. Then it is not just you, the outward man, *it is the Lord lighting the candle for you*—the inward man—the man on the inside.

"I want to ask you a question," I said to her, "so we can ascertain just which this is. From the physical, from the mental, just naturally speaking, do you want to go back there?"

"Oh, no!"

"It couldn't be you then, could it? (It would have been better to say, it couldn't have been the flesh, the natural man, the outward man.) You're not going to be thinking about doing something you don't want to do."

I saw she had the inward witness just as I did. Sometimes the inward witness is there and people don't recognize it.

"I am convinced," I told her, "that God is leading us that way. It will have to be God to open it up and get us back there. Let's just let Him do it."

He did. Within a few months, without my doing anything to work it out, I was invited to preach a week in that church. Afterwards, the board asked if I would be interested in coming back to pastor.

I didn't tell them I had something from God. I just said, "I might be."

They said, "We have all been talking and the church wants you back."

"Well," I said, "they would have to vote on me. So I'll tell you what I'll do—just go ahead and vote, and I will tell you afterwards."

From the natural standpoint my wife and I still did not want to go back there. Although we loved the people, we did not want to live in that town. We did not want to live in that house. In my heart I wanted to obey God, but everything about my flesh recoiled. In my natural man, my outward man, and in my own natural human thinking and mind, I did not want to go back there.

So really, as I kept praying and fasting while the church board was making all the proper announcements and advertising the election, I was actually saying to the Lord that I didn't want to trust that inward witness I knew both my wife and I had.

I was over into the third day of a fast. I wanted the Lord to move in some *spectacular* way—I wanted some kind of a word, tongues and interpretation, a prophecy, or God just to write up in the sky, "GO TO THAT PLACE." I was on my knees bawling and squawling and begging—because I didn't know any better.

God also leads by an inward voice as well as by an inward witness. That inward voice said, "Get up from there and quit acting like that."

I got up. Then I said, "Lord, if You could just give me some supernatural sign, I would feel better about this." He said, "You have all I am going to give you. You don't need any supernatural sign. You don't need any supernatural writing in the sky. You don't need any tongues and interpretation. You don't need any prophecy. You know on the inside of you what to do. Now do it."

I said, "Okay, I will."

Many times we ignore the inward witness. We want something out in the sense realm. We seek the sensational and miss the supernatural.

Let's learn that God leads all of His children, *primarily*, by the inward witness.

CHAPTER 11

Number Two:
The Inward Voice

I say the truth in Christ, I lie not,
my conscience also bearing me witness in the Holy Ghost.
—Romans 9:1

The number one way the Spirit guides us is through the inward witness. Number two is by the inward voice.

The inward man, who is a spirit man, has a voice—just as the outward man has a voice. We call this voice of the inward man *conscience*. We call this voice the *still small voice.*

Your spirit has a voice. Your spirit will speak to you.

In September 1966 we moved to Tulsa, Oklahoma, from Garland, Texas, a suburb of Dallas. We had lived there 17 years. The move came about like this: My wife and I were in Tulsa on business. The ministry was growing and I had already figured out in my head what I would do with my office and home in Texas to accommodate the growth. But a friend with whom we were staying in Tulsa, said, "Brother Hagin, you ought to move to Tulsa. Brother T.L. Osborn's old office building is for sale. His business manager asked me to sell it for them." Then he quoted their price. It was extremely low. But I was not interested. Finally, he said, "Let's go look at it." I went along just to humor him.

The minute I stood inside that building a buzzer went off inside of me. (Sometimes that inward witness is so real it can almost sound like an inward "buzzer.") I knew as well as I knew my name, *this is it!* But I didn't want to listen to it; I wanted to stay in Garland.

(That's why we don't hear a lot of times. We don't want to hear. We say we do, but we don't.)

Back at our friend's home, my wife asked me about the building.

"Oh, no. I've already got it all figured out. We'll stay where we are. We'll turn our whole home into an office. And we'll just stay in Garland."

We went to bed that night, but I couldn't sleep.

Ordinarily, I have no trouble sleeping. The Bible says, "*. . . he giveth his beloved sleep*" (Ps. 127:2). I am His beloved. So are you. "*. . . he hath made us accepted in the beloved*" (Eph. 1:6). So I always claim the promise of God and say, "Lord, I'm Your beloved. So I take You at Your Word. I thank You for sleep." And I always go to sleep.

But this time, I couldn't. My conscience was hurting. My conscience is the voice of my spirit. My spirit knows I didn't listen to it.

Lying there quietly in the nighttime, I said, "Lord, if you want me to move to Tulsa, I will. In the natural, I don't want to move there, but I wouldn't want to stand in Your way."

Then on the inside of me I heard the still small voice. Now I'm not talking about the Spirit of God speaking. When the Holy Spirit speaks it is more authoritative. The still small voice is the voice of our own spirit speaking. But our own spirit picks it up from the Holy Spirit Who is in us. *Yes. Amen.*

That still small voice, that inward voice, not authoritative, just something on the inside of me said, "I am going to give you that building,"

I laughed. I know there is a lot of unbelief about this, but I said, "Okay. When you do, I'll believe it."

That inward voice, picking up on what the Holy Spirit was saying, said, "You watch me."

Without going into all the details, it would surprise you how God gave us that building.

[Brother Hagin gives further details of his move to Tulsa in Appendix 3.—Ed.]

CHAPTER *12*

Effects of the Spirit's Indwelling

And Paul, earnestly beholding the council, said, Men and brethren,
I have lived in all good conscience before God until this day.

—Acts 23:1

It is interesting to go through the Epistles Paul wrote to the Church and see what he said about his conscience. You will notice that he always obeyed it.

Is your conscience a safe guide?

Yes, if your spirit has become a new man in Christ, it is because your conscience is the voice of your spirit.

2 CORINTHIANS 5:17

17 Therefore if any man be in Christ, he is a new creature: old things are passed away; behold, all things are become new.

These things take place in man's spirit, in the inward man. He is first a new creature—a brand-new man in Christ. Second, old things have passed away—the nature of the devil in his spirit is gone. Third, ALL things have become new *in his spirit*—not in his body or in his mind—now he has the nature of God in his spirit.

Therefore, if your spirit is a new man with the life and nature of God in it, it is a safe guide.

A person who has not been born again could not follow the voice of his spirit. His spirit is unregenerate. His conscience would permit him to do anything.

When you have the life and nature of God in you, your conscience will not permit you to do just anything. And if you are born again, you have the life of God.

JOHN 3:16

16 For God so loved the world, that he gave his only begotten Son, that whosoever believeth in him should not perish, but have EVERLASTING LIFE.

ROMANS 6:23

23 For the wages of sin is death; but the gift of God is ETERNAL LIFE through Jesus Christ our Lord.

Someone said, "That just means we are going to live forever up in Heaven."

No, it does not only mean that. Consider this scripture:

1 JOHN 5:13

13 These things have I written unto you that believe on the name of the Son of God; that ye may know that YE HAVE ETERNAL LIFE. . . .

Have is present tense. We have *eternal life* now. If you are a born-again Christian, you have the *life of God* in your spirit now. You have the *nature* of God in your spirit now.

Oh! If people would learn to follow their spirits! If they would learn to take advantage of the life that is in them!

I joined the church and was baptized early in life—but that didn't make me a Christian. My spirit was still unregenerate when I became totally bedfast with a heart condition at the age of 15. I was truly born again during the 16 months I was bedfast. Then in August 1934, as a Baptist boy reading Grandma's Methodist Bible, I was healed.

I went back to high school. I had missed one school year. Before I was born again, I just barely got by in some classes. Back then, if you made a "D" it was failing. And if you failed one subject you stayed in that grade and took the whole thing over again. Two teachers in two subjects said to me, "We gave you two points or you would have had a 'D.'"

But after I was born again, I never made anything but a straight "A" report card. And I never took one book home to study.

Now I didn't know a thing about the baptism of the Holy Spirit then, but do you know what I did know? I knew I had the life of God in me!

As I walked down the street to school every morning, I had a conversation with the Lord. Unconsciously, I was being led by the Spirit; my heart told me to do it, and I listened to my heart instead of my head.

I said, "Now, Lord, I read in the Old Testament where Daniel and the three Hebrew children were in school in Babylon and You gave them favor with the dean of the school (Dan. 1:9). God, give me favor with every teacher. Thank You for it; I have it now. I also read, that when their three years of training were over, the three Hebrew children were 10 times smarter than the rest (vv. 18–20). Lord, I have Your life in me. John 1:4 says, *'In him was life; and the life was the light of men.'* Light stands for development. Impart to me knowledge and skill in all learning and wisdom that I may be ten times better. . . ."

Every day as I walked to school I would confess, "In Him was life and the life was the light of men. That life is in me. The life of God is in me. That life is the light—it is the development of me. It is developing my spirit. It is developing my mentality. I have God in me. I have God's wisdom in me. I have God's life in me. That life of God in my spirit dominates me. I purpose in my heart to walk in the light of life."

Now I do not mean that I just skipped by. In study hall periods at school I studied. I listened intently in class to everything that was said. But by receiving eternal life into my spirit, and getting my mind renewed with the Word, my mentality was increased from 30 to 60 percent.

The life of God will do that for anyone.

The most amazing miracle I have ever seen of eternal life affecting someone's mentality occurred in a girl I'll call Mary. Her mentality was increased by at least 90 percent.

Mary started to school at seven and went seven years without getting out of the first grade. In those seven years she never learned to write her name. Finally, they asked her parents to take her out of school.

In the church I pastored, Mary was at that time 18 years old, although she behaved like a two-year-old. She would get down and crawl around on the floor like a baby. If she happened not to be sitting with her mother, she would slide under the pews, or lift up her skirt and step over them to get to where her mother was. Her clothes were always a sight. Her hair was never combed.

Then one night during an evangelistic revival meeting, Mary came to the altar. There she received eternal life—the nature of God. A drastic change occurred instantly. The very next night she sat in the service and behaved like any other 18-year-old young lady. She had fixed her hair and dressed up. Her mentality seemed to have increased overnight.

Years later I was back in the city to help with a funeral. "What ever happened to Mary?" I asked the church secretary. She led me out on the front porch.

"See all those new houses going up out there."

I said, "Yes."

"That's an addition to the city Mary is building that. She's a widow now. She handles all her own money. She is her own financier. She has three lovely children. They are on the front pew every Sunday. They are the best dressed, and the most well-mannered children in church. As church secretary I can tell you that Mary's tithes and offerings are here every Sunday."

The life of God came into her!

I am convinced we have never completely learned what we have received. Most of us have thought that the Lord just forgave us, saying that we're the same old creature we always were. We'll just try to hold out faithful till the end. If we get enough people to pray for us, maybe we can make it.

No, thank God, the life of God has been imparted into our spirits! The nature of God is in our spirits. The Holy Spirit is living and abiding in our spirits.

CHAPTER 13

Two Experiences

*Then Philip went down to the city of Samaria and preached Christ
unto them . . . when they believed Philip preaching the things concerning the
kingdom of God, and the name of Jesus Christ, they were baptized,
both men and women . . . Now when the apostles which were at Jerusalem
heard that Samaria had received the word of God, they sent unto them
Peter and John: Who, when they were come down,
prayed for them, that they might receive the Holy Ghost:
(For as yet he was fallen upon none of them:
only they were baptized in the name of the Lord Jesus.)
Then laid they their hands on them, and they received the Holy Ghost.*

—Acts 8:5,12,14–17

Under the New Covenant every child of God has the
Spirit of God. If you are born again, the Spirit of God
is in your spirit.

We do need to differentiate between being born of the Spirit and being filled with the Spirit. The born-again Christian can be *filled* with the same Spirit that he already has in him. And when he is *filled* with that Spirit, there will be an overflowing. He will speak with other tongues as the Spirit gives him utterance (Acts 2:4).

Bible scholars know that water is a type of the Spirit of God. Jesus Himself used water as a type of the Spirit. He used it as a type of the New Birth when talking to the woman at the well of Samaria.

JOHN 4:10–11,13–14

10 Jesus answered and said unto her, If thou knewest the gift of God, and who it is that saith to thee, Give me to drink; thou wouldest have asked of him, and he would have given thee living water. *Holy Spirit*

11 The woman saith unto him, Sir, thou hast nothing to draw with, and the well is deep: from whence then hast thou that living water?

13 Jesus answered and said unto her, Whosoever drinketh of this water shall thirst again:

14 But whosoever drinketh of the water that I shall give him shall never thirst; but the water that I shall give him shall be in him a well of water springing up into everlasting life.

Jesus also used water as a type of the Spirit in the infilling of the Holy Spirit:

JOHN 7:37–39

37 In the last day, that great day of the feast, Jesus stood and cried, saying, If any man thirst, let him come unto me, and drink.

38 He that believeth on me, as the scripture hath said, out of his belly shall flow rivers of living water.

39 (But this spake he of the Spirit, which they that believe on him should receive: for the Holy Ghost was not yet given; because that Jesus was not yet glorified.)

These are two different experiences. The New Birth is a well of water in you, springing up into everlasting life. The infilling of the Holy Spirit is rivers—not just one river. The water in the well is for one purpose. The water in the well is for your own benefit. It blesses you. The water in the rivers is for another purpose. The rivers flowing out of you bless someone else.

Some people say, "If you are born of the Spirit, you have the Spirit, and that's all there is." But, no, just because you have had one drink of water is no sign you're full of water. There is the experience subsequent to the New Birth of being filled with the Spirit—and as a result, out of the belly (the innermost being—the spirit) rivers of living water can flow.

Others say that people who are not filled with the Spirit speaking with other tongues do not have the Holy Spirit. That is not true. If I drink half a glass of water, I may not be full, but at least I have water in me. If one is born of the Spirit of God, he has the Spirit of God abiding in him.

Must even born again of the Spirit must be filled with the Holy Spirit

55

CHAPTER *14*

God Inside

. . . for ye are the temple of the living God; as God hath said,
I will dwell in them, and walk in them;
and I will be their God, and they shall be my people.

—2 Corinthians 6:16

If you are born again, the Holy Spirit is living and abiding in your spirit.

He's living and abiding where? In your head? No. In your body? In a sense, yes, but not exactly in the way we might think. The only reason your body becomes the temple of the Holy Spirit is because your body is the temple of your own spirit. The Holy Spirit abides in your *spirit*. And He communicates with you through your spirit.

He does not communicate directly with your mind—He is not in your mind. He is in your spirit—He communicates with you through your spirit. Of course, your spirit does reach and influence your mentality.

Even as a newborn babe in Christ, still bedfast, I would know things by an inward witness. I knew nothing about being filled with the Holy Ghost and speaking with other tongues—but I was born of the Spirit. I had the witness of the Spirit right on the inside of me that I was a child of God.

I had been bedfast about four months when my mother came to my bed one day and said, "Son, I hate to bother you, but something is wrong with Dub."

Dub is my oldest brother. He was 17 at the time and he was gone. We didn't know exactly where he was.

She sensed something in her spirit. She thought maybe he had gotten into trouble and was in jail. She said, "I've been praying for him for three days, but I need some help."

I said, "Momma, I thought you already had enough problems with me being bedfast. I've known that myself about Dub for several days. He's not in jail, though. It's not that kind of trouble. His physical life is in danger. But I've already prayed, and he will make it. His life will be spared. I've already got the answer."

I didn't know how to get the answer on healing right then—it was a year later before I was healed. But I knew some things, praise God, and God will meet you as far as your faith goes.

Three days later, Dub came home in the nighttime. You see, it was 1933 and there was no work. Men were out on the streets with no jobs in those great Depression Days. Dub had gone down to the Rio Grande Valley to look for work. He didn't find any. So he decided to hop a freight train—lots of people were riding the rails in those days—from the backside of the Valley right on through to McKinney.

About 50 miles south of Dallas a railway detective knocked him in the head and threw him off that train while it was going 50 or 60 miles an hour. He went sailing down the track. They burned coal in those days and they would put the cinders along the track. He hit those cinders and went scooting on his back. It's a wonder it hadn't broken his back. It would have if we hadn't known about it by the inward witness and prayed.

He lay out in the ditch, and then came to after a while. His shirt was completely torn off, and the seat of his britches was torn out, so he could only travel at night. In the daytime he hid out in the trees in the field—it was the time of year he could find fruit—and during the nighttime he walked up the rail toward McKinney. It was night when he got home. Momma put him to bed and he was all right in a few days.

Momma and I were not Spirit-filled Christians—but we were Christians. And we had a witness in our spirits that something was wrong—an inward intuition. This is something every Christian ought to have. It is something every Christian should develop. We should develop our spirits.

In less than 10 years' time a Full Gospel minister friend of mine was in three serious automobile accidents. People were killed. His wife was almost killed. He was seriously injured. Cars were demolished. But they were both healed by the mercy of God.

He heard me teach along some of these lines and he said to me, "Brother Hagin, every one of those accidents could have been avoided if I had listened to that inward intuition."

Yet in similar instances people will say, "I don't know why that happened to such a good Christian. He's a preacher." (Preachers have to learn to listen to their spirits just like you have to learn to listen to your spirit.) Then they lay it off on God and say that God did it.

This preacher said to me, "If I had listened to that inward some-thing—I just had an intuition that something was about to happen—I would have waited a little bit and prayed. Instead I thought, *I'm busy. I don't have time to pray.*"

Many times, if we would have waited, God would have shown us. We could have avoided many things. But let's not moan and groan about past failures. Let's just take advantage of what is ours and see to it that it doesn't happen again. We can do nothing about what is past anyhow. Let's begin to develop our spirits, and learn to listen to them.

The Holy Spirit is abiding in your spirit. It is your spirit that picks up these things from the Holy Spirit and then passes them on to your mind by an inward intuition, or inward witness.

Jesus said, "*. . . If a man love me, he will keep my words: and my Father will love him, and we will come unto him, and make our abode with him*" (John 14:23). In this passage of scripture, Jesus is talking about the Holy Spirit's coming. Jesus and the Father in the Person of the Holy Spirit come to abide in us. An abode is the place where one lives. Another translation says, "We will come unto him, and make our home with him."

The Holy Spirit, through the Apostle Paul said, "*Know ye not that ye are the temple of God and that the Spirit of God dwelleth in you?*" (1 Cor. 3:16). Another translation says, "The Spirit of God is at home in you." That's where He lives—in you!

The Bible says, "*. . . for ye are the temple of the living God; as God hath said, I will dwell in them, and walk in them; and I will be their God, and they shall be my people*" (2 Cor. 6:16).

Put those three scriptures together:

JOHN 14:23; 1 CORINTHIANS 3:16; 2 CORINTHIANS 6:16

Jesus answered and said unto him, If a man love me, he will keep my words: and my Father will love him, and we will come unto him, and make our abode with him . . . Know ye not that ye are the temple of God, and that the Spirit of God dwelleth in you? . . . for ye are the temple of the living God; as God hath said, I will dwell in them, and walk in them; and I will be their God, and they shall be my people.

We have never yet plumbed the depth of what God is really saying: "I will dwell in them. I will live in them. I will walk in them." If God is dwelling *in* us—and He is—then that is where He will speak to us.

CHAPTER *15*

Depend on Your Spirit

For verily I say unto you, That whosoever shall say unto this mountain,
Be thou removed, and be thou cast into the sea;
and shall not doubt in his heart, but shall believe that those things
which he saith shall come to pass; he shall have whatsoever he saith.
Therefore I say unto you, What things soever ye desire, when ye pray,
believe that ye receive them, and ye shall have them.

—Mark 11:23–24

Your spirit knows things that your head does not know, because the Holy Spirit is in your spirit.

When medical science gave me up to die as a teenager and said they could do nothing further for me, I knew somehow that if there was help for me anywhere it would be in the Bible.

I started with the New Testament because I knew I didn't have much time. Eventually I came to Mark 11:23 and 24.

When I came to Mark 11:24, something from outside me somewhere said to my mind, *That doesn't mean what things soever ye desire physically, or materially, or financially. That just means whatsoever things ye desire spiritually. Healing has been done away with.*

I tried to get my pastor to come and tell me what Mark 11:24 did mean. He did not come. One preacher finally did come. He patted my hand, put on a professional voice and said, "Just be patient my boy. In a few more days it will all be over."

I accepted the verdict and lay there expecting to die. It was two months before I got back into the Bible and back to Mark 11:23 and 24.

I said, "Lord, I tried to get someone to help me and I couldn't. So I am going to tell You what I am going to do. I am just going to take You at Your Word. When You were here on earth, You said it. I am going to believe it. If You didn't lie about it, I am coming off this bed, because I can believe what You said I can believe."

Then I hit on this idea. (It took me a long time because I had limited use of my hands. They propped the Bible in front of me and I just sort of "scooted" the pages.) I decided to run my reference on *faith* and *healing*. I came to James 5:14 and 15.

JAMES 5:14–15

14 Is any sick among you? let him call for the elders of the church; and let them pray over him, anointing him with oil in the name of the Lord:

15 And the prayer of faith shall save the sick, and the Lord shall raise him up; and if he have committed sins, they shall be forgiven him.

Wow

I'm just going to take You at Your Word!

I thought all the rest of the healing scriptures and prayer promises hinged on that—I thought you HAD to call for the elders of the church. (You don't have to—you just can if you need to.) So I began to cry, "Dear Lord, if I have to call for the elders of the church to anoint me with oil to be healed, then I can't be healed. I don't know any elders of the church that believe in that."

I had been saved about six months, and I had never heard an inward voice. I am not talking about the voice of the Spirit of God—that is more authoritative—I am talking about that still small voice of my spirit.

My spirit said to me, "Did you notice that verse said that the prayer of faith shall save the sick?"

I had to look again. I'd had my mind on the elders and had missed that. "Yes," I said aloud, "that is what it says!" It came as a real shock to me.

Then on the inside of me these words were spoken, "You can pray that prayer as well as anyone can." Hallelujah!

But my spiritual education was slow—just like yours. I stayed in that bed nine more months before I finally saw that I had to believe I received my healing before it would be manifested.

It was while I was praying and saying, "I believe that I receive my healing," that I saw what I must do. I said, "I believe that I receive healing from the top of my head to the soles of my feet." Then I began to praise God because I believed that I received my healing.

Again, on the inside of me, I heard these words—this was not that authoritative voice, but just a still small voice, so faint I would not have heard it if my mind and body had been very active—"Now you believe that you are well."

I said, "I sure do."

That inward voice said, "Get up then. Well people ought to be up at 10:30 in the morning."

I had been paralyzed. It was a struggle. I pushed myself. Finally, I got up to where I was draped over the bedpost. My knees sagged down not far from the floor. I had no feeling from my waist down. But draped over that bedpost I said it again, "I want to announce in the Presence of Almighty God, the Lord Jesus Christ, the Holy Spirit, and the holy angels present in this room, and I want to call the devil to record and all evil spirits that may be present in this room, that according to Mark 11:24, I believe that I receive my healing."

When I said that, physically, I felt something. It felt like someone above me was pouring a pitcher of honey on me. I felt it strike me on the top of my head. It seemed to pile up like honey would, and then it began to ooze down over me. It had a warm glow to it. It spread down over my head, down my neck and shoulders, down my arms and out the ends of my fingers, and down my body and out the ends of my toes.

All of a sudden I was standing straight! I have been straight ever since.

But I want you to see this. I listened to my spirit. Faith is of the spirit. Your faith will not work to its fullest until you learn some of these things. Learn to depend on Him—the One Who is in you. Learn to develop your own spirit. Have faith in the fact that *your* faith in God works.

CHAPTER 16

Tenderhearted

*For if our heart condemn us, God is greater than our heart
and knoweth all things. Beloved, if our heart condemn us not,
then have we confidence toward God.*

—1 John 3:20–21

Does the Holy Spirit condemn you if you do wrong as a Christian?

No. It is your spirit that condemns you.

You need to learn that. It's a hard lesson to learn, however, because we have been taught incorrectly.

The Holy Spirit will not condemn you. Why? Because God won't. Study what the Holy Spirit through Paul wrote in the Epistle to the Romans. He asked: Who is it that condemns? Does God condemn? No, it is God that justifies.

Jesus said that the only sin the Holy Spirit will convict the world of is the sin of rejecting Jesus (John 16:7–9).

It is your own conscience—the voice of your own spirit—that knows when you have done wrong.

I have found that even when I do wrong, though my spirit condemns me, the Holy Spirit is there to comfort me, to help me, to show me the way back. You will never read in the Bible where the Holy Spirit is a condemner. Jesus called Him *the Comforter*. The seven-fold meaning of that word from the Greek is brought out in *The Amplified Bible*:

JOHN 14:16 (*Amplified*)

16 And I will ask the Father, and He will give you another Comforter (Counselor, Helper, Intercessor, Advocate, Strengthener and Standby) that He may remain with you forever.

The Holy Spirit is all of those! He will stand by you when no one else will. He will help you. He is a Helper! It is your own spirit that knows the moment you have done wrong. I am glad I learned that early. It has paid off richly for me in life.

I was barely saved and healed and back in high school when the following incident occurred: I really don't know why it slipped out— no one in our family used profanity. But we had a neighbor, bless his heart, who could—as we say in Texas—"cuss up a storm." You could hear him all over our end of town. I suppose I picked it up from him. Anyway, I simply said to one of the boys, "Hell, no (something or other)."

The minute I said that I knew on the inside it was wrong. What was it that condemned me? the Holy Spirit? No. It was my spirit. My spirit, this new creature, this new man doesn't talk that way. The Life and Nature of God doesn't talk that way. Now the flesh, the outward man, may want to go on doing some things that he did before, and talking in ways he talked before, but you have to crucify the flesh. A good way to crucify the flesh—the outward man—is to bring your mistakes right out in the open.

I did that right then. I didn't wait until I was moved. In my heart I said, "Dear God, forgive me for saying that." The young man I said it to had walked away. I located him and asked him to forgive me. He hadn't noticed what I'd said; he was used to people talking that way. But I had to get it right.

It was the voice of my spirit. It was my conscience. My conscience was tender, and I didn't want to violate it. *Unless you keep a tender conscience, spiritual things will be indistinct to you.* That's because your conscience is the voice of your spirit and it is your conscience—the voice of your spirit—that will relate to your mind what the Spirit of God is saying to you down in your heart.

The Bible speaks about Christians even having their conscience seared:

1 TIMOTHY 4:2

2 Speaking lies in hypocrisy; having their conscience seared with a hot iron.

The first church I pastored was a community church out in the country. I usually went out Saturday night, spent Saturday and Sunday nights, and came back into town on Monday. I stayed quite often in the home of a dear Methodist man. This fine spiritual man, a great man really, was 89 years old. He and I didn't get up as early as the others did on his farm. They would be out doing chores or be out working in the field when this older gentleman and I had breakfast together about 8 o'clock.

I didn't drink coffee, but this old gentleman did. Now you could scarcely believe it unless you saw it, but he had one of those old-fashioned coffee pots—this was the mid-30's—sitting on an old-fashioned wood stove with coffee boiling in it. I have seen him take that boiling coffee, pour it into a big thick mug—and when it was still so hot it simmered in that mug—turn it up to his mouth, and drink the whole cup.

The first time I saw him do it, I hollered. I felt like my mouth and throat were burning.

How could he do that? I couldn't. The tissues of my lips, the inside of my mouth, my throat and esophagus are so tender, just one tea-spoonful would have burned all the way down. But he drank a whole mug without taking it away from his mouth.

He couldn't do that to begin with though. Through years of drinking coffee that hot, his lips and mouth, and throat and esophagus became seared. Eventually, he could drink it that hot, and it didn't bother him.

Spiritually, the same thing can happen.

Learn to keep a tender conscience. Learn the minute you miss it and your conscience condemns you, to correct it right then. Don't wait until you go to church. Immediately say, "Lord, forgive me. I missed it." If you have to, if someone else saw or heard you, tell that person right away, "I did wrong. Please forgive me. I shouldn't have said that."

You will have to keep your spirit tender if you are going to be led by the Spirit.

CHAPTER *17*

Feelings: The Voice of the Body

The Spirit itself [Himself] *beareth witness with our spirit. . . .*

—Romans 8:16

Too often people think that the witness this verse is talking about is a physical something. It is not. It is a spiritual something. It is the Spirit of God bearing witness with our spirits. He does not bear witness with our bodies. You cannot go by physical feeling.

We confuse things by the way we talk. We say, "I feel God's Presence." No, we don't. We sense His Presence spiritually. Use the word *feeling* advisedly; it leaves the wrong impression that it is a physical feeling. Don't mix the physical with it.

Feeling is the voice of the body.

Reason is the voice of the soul, or the mind.

Conscience is the voice of the spirit.

To go by *feeling* is to get into trouble. That is the reason so many Christians are up and down (I call them yo-yo Christians), and in and out. They go by their feelings. They don't walk by faith. They don't walk by their spirits.

When they feel good, they say, "Glory to God, I'm saved. Hallelujah, I'm filled with the Spirit. Everything is fine." When they feel bad, their faces are long and they say, "I've lost it all. I don't feel like I did, so I must be backslidden."

I hear people, bless their hearts, talking about being in the valley, then being on the mountaintop, then getting back down in the valley again. I have never been in the valley. I have been saved more than fifty years and I have never been anywhere but on the mountaintop. You do not have to get down in the valley.

People talk about "valley experiences." I have never had any valley experiences. Oh, yes, there have been tests and trials, but I was on the mountaintop all the time, shouting my way through—living above the tests and the trials!

A woman we had pastored in years gone by came to a meeting where we were and told us about her 39-year-old daughter. They were about to operate on her when they discovered she had a tumor. Then they also found through hospital tests that she was a diabetic. They were trying to get the diabetic condition under control when she went into a coma. Three doctors said she would never regain consciousness; she would die.

This mother said, "Will you lay your hands on this handkerchief?" I did, and we prayed. Then that mother got on a bus and rode 300 miles back to the hospital where her daughter lay unconscious. She reached under the oxygen tent and laid the handkerchief on her daughter's chest. The minute it touched her, she revived. She was healed, born again, filled with the Holy Spirit and began to speak in tongues, all in one application.

The nurses got excited and called the doctor. The doctor said, "This is wonderful that she has regained consciousness. But she must remain quiet." He gave her a shot to quiet her down—but it never did take effect. She just kept on speaking in tongues and shouting, "I'm healed. I'm healed. I'm healed."

The next day they began to run tests. Her blood was perfect. She no longer had diabetes. Then they couldn't find the tumor. It had disappeared. After several days they dismissed her.

This woman told my wife and me sometime later that the doctor said, "We won't charge you anything. We didn't do anything. A Higher Power than us did it."

Now, three years later, when she was 42 years old, her sister brought her to our door at 2 o'clock one morning. She had another tumor.

I thought she had come to be healed. So I said, "You can be healed again. We will just lay hands on you."

She said, with tears, "Brother Hagin, I don't really care whether I get healed or not. Really, if I could just get back to where I was with God I would just as soon die and go on to Heaven."

When she said this, I assumed she must have backslidden. She looked so sad, I just knew she must have committed some terrible sin. So I said, "The Lord will forgive you . . ." And I went through what the Bible says about that. Then I said, "We'll all just kneel down here by the couch. (My wife and the woman's sister were there too.) I will kneel beside you. Now you don't have to confess to me, but tell the Lord about it and He will forgive you."

She looked up at me and said, "Brother Hagin, I've searched my heart, and as far as I know, I haven't done anything wrong."

I got aggravated. I'd gotten to bed late—I was driving a distance and holding meetings every night. And just right in the middle of good sound sleep, early in the morning, came this knocking at the door that woke us. I guess I did speak sharply to her; I know I did.

I said, "Get up from the floor. Sit down there on that couch." I was disgusted. "If you haven't done anything wrong, what in the world makes you think you have to get back to God?"

"Well," she said, "I don't feel like I used to."

I said, "What has that got to do with it? If I were going by feeling, half the time when I get up to preach I would announce that I must be backslidden."

She looked at me. "Do you mean preachers are that way too?"

I said, "Yes, we're just as human as anyone else. In fact, if I were going by feelings right now, I would be having you pray for me. I don't feel a thing. I haven't felt a thing since you got here."

She said, "What do you do then? How do you pray through?"

I said, "I don't pray through. I'm already through. A Christian ought to walk through—he ought to be *through*—living in fellowship with God, every day, every minute, every hour."

She said, "What do you do then?"

"Well," I said, "just sit there and watch me. I'm going to close my eyes and pray, but you keep your eyes open."

Then I prayed, "Dear Lord, I'm so glad that I'm a child of God. I'm so glad I'm saved. I'm so glad I have been born again. I don't feel anything—but that has nothing to do with it. My inward man is a new man. My inward man is a new creature in Christ. I want to thank You that not only am I born again—but I'm filled with the Holy Spirit.

God the Father, God the Son, and God the Holy Spirit reside in me. I want to thank You for that. Hallelujah!"

I didn't feel anything, but I said it anyhow. Then, when I confessed that, in my spirit (He was in there all the time) something began to bubble up inside of me. It was a move and manifestation of the Spirit of God. I still did not feel anything, but in my spirit I could sense that bubbling. It got up in my throat. I began to laugh—there is a laugh in the Spirit. I began to speak in tongues.

This lady said, "The expression on your face changed. Your face just lit up."

I said, "That was in there all the time. Paul told Timothy to stir up the gift that was in him. I just stirred up what I had in me all the time."

She said, "Can I do that?"

I said, "Yes, you can."

She did—she stirred up what was in her all the time.

I do not remember even praying about the tumor. The last account I had of her, it had disappeared.

Base your faith on the Word—not on your feelings. Romans 8:16 does not say that the Spirit beareth witness with our bodies, or with our feelings.

Smith Wigglesworth, the great English apostle of faith, said, "I am not moved by what I feel. I am not moved by what I see. I am moved only by what I believe. I cannot understand God by feelings. I understand God by what the Word says about Him. I understand the Lord Jesus Christ by what the Word says about Him. He is everything the Word says He is."

You cannot understand yourself by feelings. Understand yourself as a born-again, Spirit-filled Christian by what the Word of God says

All three in both heads me (top)

you. And when you read what the Word says about you—then, whether you feel like it or not, say, "Yes, that's me. I have that. The Word says I have that. I can do what the Word says I can do. I am what the Word says I am."

You will begin to develop spiritually then. *Amen.*

And it is with your spirit that the Holy Spirit bears witness.

Confess it until you believe it not feel it!

CHAPTER 18

Help From Within

*Howbeit when he, the Spirit of truth, is come, he will guide you
into all truth: for he shall not speak of himself; but whatsoever he shall hear,
that shall he speak: and he will shew you things to come.*

—John 16:13

Let's notice some things Jesus said about the Holy Spirit in John 16:13. *". . . he will guide you into all truth. . . ."* He will lead you. He will guide you.

". . . for he shall not speak of himself; but whatsoever he shall hear, that shall he speak. . . ." The Holy Spirit does speak. Whatever He hears God say, whatever He hears Jesus say, He will speak to your spirit. Where is He to speak? He is in your spirit, and that is where He speaks. He doesn't speak out in the air somewhere. He speaks on the inside. The Holy Spirit passes God's message on to your spirit, either

by an inward witness, by the still small voice—the voice of your conscience, or by an inward voice which is the more authoritative voice of the Holy Spirit.

"*. . . he will shew you things to come. . . .*" I do not believe this just means that the Holy Spirit will show us about future events as recorded in the Word of God. It also means that the Holy Spirit will show *you* things to come. In my own individual life, for instance, there has never been a death in our close family that I did not know about in advance. I knew two years ahead of time that my father-in-law was going to die, so I began to prepare my wife for his death. She was his only daughter, the baby of the family, and very close to her father. I knew she would take it hard. So I began to say to her, "Honey, you know Mr. Rooker is getting older. Then over the next two years I dropped a word here and there, just getting her ready.

I was away in a meeting when the telephone call came. After the service one night, I was sitting in the hotel. The phone rang. Something in me said, "That's for you. This is what you have been talking about for two years now." Within twenty-eight days he was in Heaven. You are not unprepared when you know things ahead of time.

JOHN 14:26

26 But the Comforter, which is the Holy Ghost, whom the Father will send in my name, he shall teach you all things, and bring all things to your remembrance, whatsoever I have said unto you.

❶ *The Holy Spirit shall teach you.*

❶ *He shall bring all things to your remembrance.*

People often ask me how I remember things. At one time I could quote three-fourths of the New Testament.

Wow!

"How do you memorize scripture?"

I always answer, "I never memorized scripture in my life. I know nothing about memorization. I suppose you could develop your mind if you worked at it. But I just get to talking and it rises up in me. The Holy Spirit brings it to my remembrance. He is inside of me."

The Holy Spirit will show you things to come and bring things to your remembrance if you will learn to cooperate with Him.

I Love Him.

CHAPTER *19*

Number Three: The Voice of the Holy Spirit

While Peter thought on the vision, the Spirit said unto him,
Behold, three men seek thee.

—Acts 10:19

God leads us by what we call the still small voice. But He also leads us by the voice of the Spirit of God speaking to us. This is the third way we are led by the Spirit. Number one is by the inward witness. Number two is by the inward still small voice. Number three is by the more authoritative voice of the Holy Spirit.

There is a difference between the inward voice of the Holy Spirit speaking to our spirits, and that still small voice which is the voice of our own spirit speaking to us. When the Holy Spirit within you speaks, it is more authoritative.

Sometimes it is so real it almost seems to be an audible voice; you may even look around to see who said it. It may seem so audible sometimes that you may think someone behind you said something. But then you realize it was *in* you.

Remember in the Old Testament how the young boy Samuel heard a voice call his name, "Samuel, Samuel?" He thought Eli was calling him. He jumped up and ran to Eli to find out what he wanted. Eli said, "No, I didn't call you." Samuel went back to bed. Then again he heard, "Samuel, Samuel." Again he ran to Eli. "No, I didn't call you." It happened the third time. Finally, it dawned on Eli what was happening. Eli said, "The next time the Lord calls you, answer Him." So the next time it happened, Samuel answered that voice, and the Lord spoke further to him (1 Sam. Chapter 3).

All of God's leadings are supernatural; some, however, are not so spectacular. But I have found in more than 50 years of ministry that when God moved in a more spectacular way—when He has spoken to me in what seemed to me to be an audible voice—it meant there was rough sailing ahead. If He had not spoken so spectacularly I would not have stayed steady.

Concerning the last church I pastored, for example, I heard the pastorate was open and I made arrangements to preach there one Wednesday night. During the period of time before I was to go there to preach, I held a three-week revival in Houston. During this revival, the pastor, his brother (who was also a preacher), and I met at the church every day to pray about the night services. The church with the open pastorate was their home church. Every day the pastor and his brother would ask me, "Have you prayed about that church yet?"

Finally, I did pray about it. I just said to the Lord, "I'm going up to that church next Monday and I'm going to preach Wednesday. I don't know whether You want me to pastor there or not. I don't know if I even want to pastor it. But whatever You say about it is fine with me."

That is all I said. Then I heard a voice speak so plainly, I jumped. I looked behind me. I really thought that one of the preachers had heard me pray and was joking with me, because I heard this voice, and to me it was audible. The voice said, "You are the next pastor at that church, and that will be the last church you will ever pastor."

(You could interpret that a thousand different ways! You could let the devil tell you that you were going to die, or that you were going to be defeated. But it actually meant that my ministry would change to a field ministry.)

About then those two preachers walked down the aisle. As usual, they asked, "Have you prayed about that church yet?"

I said, "You two fellows are looking at the next pastor."

"Oooh, if you knew that church like we know it, you wouldn't say that. It's split right down the middle. Anything half the church is for, the other half is against. It takes two-thirds of the vote to get elected as pastor, and we'll just be honest with you, you won't be able to get elected."

"I don't know about that. I just know I'm the next pastor."

"Well, you don't know that church like we do."

I said, "No, but I know Jesus. And I know the Spirit of God. I know what He said to me."

After I preached the first time, I saw why God moved in such a spectacular way. Every word I spoke bounced right back to me like a rubber ball bouncing off the back wall. It was tough.

I thought I was only going to preach one night, but they had made arrangements for me to preach several nights. Each night my wife and children and I had to move to a different place to stay. We were at one deacon's house one night, and another deacon's house the next night.

One deacon told us, "If you stayed with me all the time, some of the rest of the congregation would probably get jealous and think I'm for you and they would vote against you."

We kept all our things in the car, and every night we would get out just enough for the next day. And every night when we got off to bed, I would say to my wife, "If God hadn't spoken so spectacularly to me, I would just get up, get the children, get into the car, and leave without saying a word to anyone."

My flesh wanted to leave so badly. My mind wanted to leave. My spirit held me steady because God had spoken to me in such a spectacular way.

They had the election. I got every vote. Everyone said, "It's the greatest miracle of the century—that anyone could get that kind of vote from this church."

I knew all the time I would get it. The Spirit of God had told me I would.

CHAPTER 20

Judging by the Word

Prove all things. . . .

—1 Thessalonians 5:21

Always remember this: the Bible teaches that the Spirit of God and the Word of God agree. Anytime the Spirit of God speaks to you, it will always be in line with the Word.

People have heard "voices" and have gotten every kind of "revelation" you can imagine. Some people are always claiming to hear a voice.

You can, and you should, judge these things. You can judge whether spiritual experiences are right or wrong simply by judging them by the Word.

Several years ago I was preaching in California. A woman who had invited the pastor, his wife, and me to her home for the noon meal said, "Brother Hagin, I want to tell you what the Lord said to me. I want to give you my *revelation*."

Before she opened her mouth I sensed by the inward witness in my spirit that something was not right. But she persisted, and I agreed to listen. She had fed us in her lovely home, and now she wanted to give me this "revelation." She began to relate it and she talked for about ten minutes before I stopped her. I just couldn't stand anymore.

"Please," I said, "wait a minute. There's a Bible there on the table by the chair. Pick it up and open it to _____." I gave her a chapter and verse in the New Testament. "Read that."

She read it. Then I gave her another verse of scripture. She read it. I pointed her to several scriptures. Everything she read contradicted what she said.

I said, "See, I cannot accept what you are saying. It is not in line with this Book. Therefore it cannot be the Spirit of God."

"But, Brother Hagin, I was praying at the altar."

I said, "I don't care if you were praying on top of the church. It's still not right. It is not in line with the Word."

"Yes, but I know God gave this to me."

I said, "No, He didn't. This is His Word and what you are saying is in direct opposition to what the Word of God says. Can you give me any scripture to substantiate what you are saying?"

"No. But I know I heard this voice speak to me."

"I just gave you five scriptures, and with a little thought I could have given you twenty, that contradict what you are saying."

"Well, yes," she said, "but Bible or no Bible, I know God spoke to me and I am going to stay with it."

As we left, the pastor said to me, "I didn't want to say anything to you before, but this dear woman was a fine saint of God, on fire for the Lord. She was a blessing to the church. Now she has been put out of every Full Gospel church in the city because she persists in pushing this *revelation* off on everyone."

We are not to seek voices.

We should not follow voices.

We should follow the Word of God.

I preached a meeting in Oregon in the summer of 1954. At the close of one of the first services, I was laying hands on the people who stood in the long prayer line. I asked each one what they had come forward for before I ministered to them. When I came to one woman, her husband who had her by the arm said, "We have come for my wife's healing." He told me she'd had a mental breakdown.

I did not know this woman was a former Sunday school teacher in that church, nor that her husband was a deacon in the church.

But when I laid hands on her, in a second of time just like it ran off on a television screen, I knew all about this situation. I knew it by the spiritual gift called the word of knowledge (1 Cor. 12:8). I saw this woman in a large tent meeting in one of Oregon's largest cities. I saw her sitting in the congregation with thousands of people. She heard the evangelist tell how God spoke to him in an audible voice and called him into the ministry.

I do not doubt that. This woman failed to realize, however, that this evangelist did not ask God to speak to him that way. God just did it on His own. We have no right to seek that God would speak to us in an audible voice. If God told us He would in His Word, then all of us would have a right to claim it. But this evangelist hadn't even particularly expected God to speak in that way—but if God wants to, He can, and He saw fit to do so in that particular case.

At the time this woman heard the evangelist tell that, she was all right mentally. But then she began to seek God to speak to her in an audible voice—and the devil accommodated her. She began to hear voices. They drove her insane. She was now about to be taken to the asylum for the second time.

I also saw this in the spirit: Her husband had taken her to this same evangelist for deliverance. She did not receive deliverance. Now her husband blamed that evangelist. Then her husband had taken her to another leading evangelist. She had failed to be delivered. Now her husband was angry with that other evangelist too. I knew she would not be delivered if I laid hands on her, and then he would be angry with me. So I took my hand off of her.

I said to the man, "Take your wife into the pastor's study. Wait there. When I finish this line, I will talk with you." After we were finished with the healing line, the pastor and I went into the study together.

"First of all," I said to this couple, "I have never been to Oregon before. I have never seen you folks before. I don't even know if the pastor knows you."

The pastor said, "He's one of our deacons."

"Well," I said, "the pastor will tell you he has not told me anything."

Then I related what I had seen.

The deacon said, "That's exactly right."

"Now," I said, "I will tell you why I didn't minister to your wife. You see, she wants to hear these voices."

Then I said, "She is not that far gone mentally that she doesn't know what I am saying."

She spoke up, "I know exactly what you are saying."

I said, "Sister, you are not going to be delivered until you want to be delivered. As long as you like it the way it is—as long as you want to hear these voices—you are going to hear them."

She said, "I want to hear them."

As long as a sinner wants to live in sin, God will let him live in sin. But if he wants to change, God will meet him and deliver him.

And even though a person is a Christian, that does not mean he loses his free moral agency. He does not become a robot—a machine whereby God pushes a button and he automatically has to do whatever God desires. He is still a free moral agent. As long as he wants things like they are, they will stay that way. But if he wants to cooperate with God, he can be helped.

This woman said, "That's the way I want it."

I said, "I knew that the minute I touched you. That's the reason I didn't minister to you. As long as you want it this way, it's going to be this way."

DO NOT SEEK VOICES!

1 CORINTHIANS 14:10

10 There are, it may be, so many kinds of voices in the world, and none of them is without signification.

We are not to accept anything without examining it in the light of the Word of God.

I am glad that I learned some of these things early in life. I mentioned I received my healing as a young boy by just acting on Mark 11:23 and 24.

I was born with a deformed heart. I never ran and played as other children did. I became bedfast four months before my sixteenth birthday. My body became practically totally paralyzed. I wasted away until I weighed only 89 pounds.

One day I asked the fifth doctor on the case, "Is something wrong with my eyesight, or with my blood? When Dr. Mathis took blood from my finger, it didn't look red."

This doctor said, "I will tell you the truth, son. And I will explain it to you in layman's terms. The white blood corpuscles eat up the red corpuscles faster than you can build them up, or we, medically, can do anything about it. If you didn't have the heart condition, if you didn't have the paralysis, this incurable blood disease alone would prove fatal."

I knew nothing about divine healing. I didn't know anyone in all the world believed in divine healing. When I found it in the Bible, I thought I had found something no one else knew anything about. And I acted on God's Word and was healed.

The members of my family were what we call *nominal* Christians. Literally, they were baby Christians. They were saved, but they were not taught beyond that. They were ignorant of the Word of God concerning healing. (Our church taught God could heal, if He *would*. Others taught not only that He *would* not heal, but that He *could* not heal.) So when I began to see certain things in the Bible and began to talk to my family about them, they discouraged me. I had enough sense just to stay with the Bible and keep those things to myself.

No one was in the room when I received my healing. I had been getting up and walking around the room for a couple of days before I said to Momma, "Please bring me a pair of shoes and socks, some underclothes, and a pair of pants and a shirt. (I had worn nothing but bedclothes for 16 months.) I am going to get up and go to the breakfast table in the morning."

"Oh, son, do you know what you're doing?"

It took me 45 minutes to talk her into the notion of laying out those clothes for me.

We made our home with my grandparents on my mother's side, and I asked my mother not to tell the rest of the family.

Now you could just mark it down. Grandpa got up early and sat out on the porch swing. When you heard that porch swing creak as he got up and headed toward the back of the house to the dining room, there was no use in looking at your watch; it was 7:30. Grandpa ran on schedule. If you did look at your watch, and it didn't say 7:30, you had better set it. It was 7:30.

My bedroom was in the front of the house. At 7:30 that August morning I heard that porch swing creak. I heard his footsteps as he walked to the back of the house. I was already fully clothed, sitting in a chair in my room. I gave them time to get seated at the table. Then I walked out of my room, across another bedroom, and into the dining room.

They did not expect that. Grandpa, a man of few words, looked up and said, "Is the dead raised? Is Lazarus raised up?"

I said, "Yes, the Lord has raised me up."

Then he asked me to offer the blessing. I prayed. And we ate. It is amazing how quickly you can eat if you don't talk so much. You didn't talk at Grandpa's table— especially the young folks. Within 15 minutes we were finished.

I went back to my room. It was 10 minutes till 8 o'clock. I knew Momma would come in about 8 o'clock to make up the bed. Usually I was in it and she would give me my bath. Just two days before, the day I was healed, she had bathed me. I was that helpless. So this Thursday morning, even though my heart was beating right, I felt weak from exerting so much energy.

So I thought, *I'm just going to lie down across the bed and rest till Momma comes to clean the room. Then I'll go out and sit with Grandpa in the swing.* I had in mind to walk uptown about 10 o'clock.

I dozed off to sleep and slept ten minutes. At 8 o'clock I suddenly became wide awake. I thought Momma was in the room. Someone was in the room. I didn't see him, but I heard this voice—to me it was audible.

The voice spoke in a slow, deep monotone and even quoted scripture. It said, "AND WHAT IS YOUR LIFE? IT IS EVEN A VAPOR THAT APPEARETH FOR A TIME, AND THEN VANISHETH AWAY."

There was a pause.

Then the voice said, "AND TODAY THOU SHALT SURELY DIE."

Every voice is not God. The first audible voice I ever heard was the devil, but I didn't recognize that then. I thought God was right there in that room.

I sat up in the bed. Thoughts came into my mind faster than machine gun bullets fly. I knew James said, *"For what is your life? It is even a vapour, that appeareth for a little time, and then vanisheth away"* (James 4:14). I knew that was scripture. And I knew the Lord told Isaiah to tell Hezekiah, *"Set thine house in order: for thou shalt die, and not live"* (Isa. 38:1).

Also, for the first six months of being bedfast, before I had known about divine healing, I had prayed the only way I understood. The doctors had said I had to die and I had accepted it, so I had prayed, "Lord, just let me know ahead of time, so I will have time to tell everyone goodbye."

So when I heard this voice speaking to me, I thought *God has moved in this supernatural way to let you know you are going to die so you will have time to tell everyone good-bye. Divine healing is right. You have been healed.* (The devil couldn't argue that. I already had the

Word on that.) *Your family knows you have been healed. They can see that. But remember, the Bible said, "It is appointed unto men once to die," and your appointed time has come. You are going to die today.*

I got up off the bed and I tiptoed across the room (I thought God was standing right in that room) and I sat down in a chair by the window. There I waited, from about 8:30 in the morning until 2:30 in the afternoon, to die.

About 2:30, still sitting in that chair, some words came floating up from somewhere down inside me. I didn't know then what I know now. But I was born of the Spirit. The Holy Spirit was in my spirit. And He is the One who wrote the Bible. Holy men of old wrote as they were moved by the Spirit of God. The Holy Spirit knows what is in that Book. Because He was in me, then my spirit knew some things that the Holy Spirit knows.

So these words came floating up from somewhere inside me into my mind, *With long life will I satisfy him, and show him my salvation.*

I didn't listen to them. I just let them float away from me. I still sat there waiting to die.

The second time, these words came floating up from inside me into my mind, *With long life will I satisfy him, and show him my salvation.*

I picked them up and turned them over a couple of times in my mind. Then I thought, *Yes, but God has moved in this supernatural way to let me know I am going to die today.* When I got my mind on that, those words disappeared.

The third time, as I sat there and these words came floating up, that inward something said to my mind, *With long life will I satisfy him, and show him my salvation.*

For a moment, I picked them up and repeated them just in my mind. Then I said, in a whisper, "Yes, but God has moved in this supernatural way to let me know that I am going to die." Again, when I got my mind on that, I missed it.

The fourth time, a little more authoritatively, the Spirit of God spoke. I jumped. I thought someone had slipped up behind me. The voice of the Spirit of God said, "With long life will I satisfy him, and show him my salvation."

I said, "Who said that?" I meant, Who is in this room talking to me?

But the voice answered and said, "The 91st Psalm."

My Bible was on the floor under the chair I had been sitting in all day. I hadn't even looked at it. I picked it up now and turned to Psalm 91. When I got down to the end, sure enough, it said, *"With long life will I satisfy him, and shew him my salvation"* (v. 16).

But do you think the devil will give up that quickly? Oh, no. Another voice—it seemed like something sitting on my shoulder— said in my natural ear and mind, "Yes, but that's in the Old Testament. That's just for the Jews. That's not for the Church."

I sat there and thought for a moment. Then I said, "I know what I'll do. I will run my references. If I can find anything in the New Testament like that I will know it belongs to me and to the Church."

I started with Psalm 91. A reference to "with long life" led me into Proverbs. Then the Word began to enlighten me. In Proverbs I began to see that that first audible voice could not have been God.

The voice had quoted Hebrews 9:27, *"And as it is appointed unto men once to die, but after this the judgment,"* but had misinterpreted it. Because the devil knew I didn't know any better, the voice had said, "Everyone has an appointed time to die." You hear people say that all the time. Even born-again, Spirit-filled Christians say, "When your time comes, you're going to die." That is not true. You do not have an appointed time to die.

I read in the Book of Proverbs again and again that if you do certain things, your days will be shortened. But doing other things will add unto you length of days. I knew God's Word was right. I knew that even though that voice picked a verse out of a chapter and gave it to me, it could not have been God, because it was not in line with the rest of the Word of God.

I continued to run references. This brought me over into the New Testament. I came over to Ephesians 6:1–3. And then into First and Second Peter. And I found that Paul and Peter quoted the Old Testament concerning long life (1 Peter 3:8–12; 2 Peter 1:3).

I jumped up out of that chair with my Bible in one hand. I doubled up my fist, kicked with my foot, and said, "Devil, you get out of here. That was you talking to me. That was you that spoke to me in that supernatural voice. I want you to know that I'm not going to die today! And I'm not going to die tomorrow! And I'm not going to die next week! And I'm not going to die next month! And I'm not going to die next year! And I'm not going to die the next 5 years! And I'm not going to die the next 10 years! And I'm not going to die the next 15 years! And I'm not going to die the next 20 years! And I'm not going to die the next 25 years! And I'm not going to die the next 30 years! And I'm not going to die the next 40 years! And I'm not going to die the next 50 years! And I'm not going to die the next 55 years!

God's Word says, 'With long life will I *satisfy* thee' (Ps. 91:16) And I'm going to go on living until I'm satisfied!"

CHAPTER 21

My Spirit? The Flesh? or the Holy Spirit?

The spirit of man is the candle of the Lord. . .

—Proverbs 20:27

Someone might ask, "How can I tell whether it is my own spirit, or the Holy Spirit telling me to do something?"

The spirit of man is the candle of the Lord.

"But it may just be me wanting to do it."

Define your terms. If by "me" you mean the flesh, of course you cannot always obey the flesh. But if by "me" you mean the inward man, the real you, then it is all right to obey the inward man. Go ahead and do what he wants you to do.

If your spirit is a new creature in Christ Jesus and old things have passed away and all things are become new, and your spirit has the life and nature of God in it and the Holy Spirit in it, and your spirit is in fellowship with God—it is not going to tell you to do something that is not right. If you are a Spirit-filled Christian, your inward man has the Holy Spirit in His fullness—not in a measure, but in His fullness—making His home in you.

It is not the inward man of the Christian that wants to do wrong—it is the outward man. You ought to be able to tell whether it is the flesh wanting to do something, or the spirit. Here is a text that has been a puzzle to many:

1 JOHN 3:9

9 Whosoever is born of God doth not commit sin; for his seed remaineth in him: and he cannot sin, because he is born of God.

This is talking about the inward man. Physically we are born of human parents and we partake of their nature. Spiritually we are born of God and partake of His nature. God's nature is not the nature to do wrong.

I have missed it a lot of times as a Christian. But my inward man did not sin. He didn't even agree with me when I did sin. He tried to get me not to do it. My heart wept because I sinned. I allowed my flesh to dominate and I missed it, but my spirit never did consent to it. God's seed is in my spirit, not in my flesh.

If you continue to allow your flesh to dominate you, you will continue to miss it. If you continue to let your natural mind dominate you, and do not get your mind renewed with the Word, you will continue to miss it.

That's why Paul wrote born-again, Spirit-filled Christians at Rome and told them to do two things: First, they were to present their bodies, and second, they were to renew their minds with the Word (Rom. 12:1–2).

Until your mind is renewed with the Word of God, your flesh and your unrenewed mind will dominate your spirit. That will keep you as a baby Christian—a carnal Christian.

Paul said to the church at Corinth, *"I, brethren, could not speak unto you as unto spiritual but as unto carnal, even as unto babes in Christ"* (1 Cor. 3:1).

"For ye are yet carnal . . . " he said (v. 3). One translation says, "For you are yet body-ruled."

Then he told them, *". . . and [ye] walk as men"* (v. 3). Another translation says, "Ye walk as mere men." What did he mean? He meant they were walking and doing things just like unsaved men do.

When you get your mind renewed with the Word, then your mind will side in with your spirit instead of with your body. And the two of them—your spirit through your mind—will control your body.

My spirit will not tell me something wrong. It has the nature of God in it; it has the life of God in it; it has the love of God in it; and it has the Spirit of God in it.

2 PETER 1:4   *Divine Nature*

4 Whereby are given unto us exceeding great and precious promises: that by these ye might be partakers of the divine nature.

We are born of God. Then we feed on the Word of God. By so doing we are partakers of the divine nature, God's nature. If we have the divine nature in us, our spirit will not tell us to do something wrong.

Whatever your spirit tells you will be right.

CHAPTER *22*

I Perceive

Now when much time was spent, and when sailing was now dangerous,
because the fast was now already past,
Paul admonished them, And said unto them,
Sirs, I perceive that this voyage will be with hurt and much damage,
not only of the lading and ship, but also of our lives.

—Acts 27:9–10

Paul said, *"I perceive. . . ."* He did not say, I have a revelation. He did not say, the Lord told me. He said, "I perceive."

How did he perceive it?

By the inward witness. He did not perceive it mentally. He did not perceive it physically. In his spirit he had this witness.

A family of seven had gone out to eat. The family had not been at the restaurant very long when the father suddenly said, "Let's go home."

"Why?"

"I don't know. I just have an urge, a perception, that we should."

They rushed home. A fire had started. If they had waited, everything would have burned. But the inward witness warned them in time.

If their home had burned down, someone might have said, "God did that. He had some purpose in it."

No, we have missed it because we haven't listened on the inside—in our spirits. We have not been spirit-conscious.

You cannot find anywhere in the Bible where God causes these things to happen to teach His people something. If those on that ship had listened to Paul, they could have saved the ship and the merchandise. As it was, they lost everything and almost lost their lives. They would have lost their lives, too, if they had not started listening to Paul.

God is not an enemy! He is trying to help us! He is not working against us! He is working for us!

As we become more spirit-conscious we can learn how to better cooperate with Him.

Remember that the primary way God leads His children is by the inward witness. = I perceive

CHAPTER 23

Spectacular Guidance

Whereupon, O king Agrippa,
I was not disobedient unto the heavenly vision.

—Acts 26:19

God leads us today just like He led the first Christians. His Word works now just like it did then. It has not changed. The Spirit of God has not changed. God does not change.

The early believers did not have one Church back then, and we have another Church now. We have made a mistake in thinking that. We are in the same age they were in—the Church Age. We are in the same Church. We have the same Holy Spirit. It has seemed to us, however, that they had a whole lot we don't have. Not so.

"For as many as are led by the Spirit of God, they are the sons of God" (Rom. 8:14). There are sons of God today. And the Spirit of God is still leading sons of God.

So we look into the Acts of the Apostles and elsewhere in the Bible to see how the Spirit of God led them. At times some received guidance through a vision. Others received guidance from an angel who appeared and told them what to do.

Such phenomena, however, did not happen every day in these people's lives. They occurred once or twice in a lifetime for most. So these are not the ordinary ways God leads. We get the impression that nearly every day an angel appeared to someone and told them something. That is not so.

Too many times while God is trying to bear witness with our spirit, trying to guide us the way He said He would in His Word, we do not listen because we want something such as a vision or an angel to appear.

We have no right to seek a vision. We have no right to ask for an angel. There are no scriptures which say that we should. We do have a right to claim what the Bible promises. If God wants to send an angel, fine. If He wants to give a vision, fine.

As a young minister I did the same thing most Christians have done in the babyhood stage of their Christianity. I heard people talking about visions and angels, and I prayed something like that would happen to me. It never did.

Then I matured spiritually so that I never expected it to happen. I did not pray that it would happen. I did not expect it. But back in 1949, I was praying one day in the last church I pastored. I had shut myself up in the church to wait on God because I had a witness in my spirit that I should do so. Then the Holy Spirit—not my spirit—spoke to me.

Before I tell you what He said, look at the following passage of scripture with me and see how Peter saw a vision and then was led by the voice of the Spirit of God:

ACTS 10:9–11

9 On the morrow, as they went on their journey, and drew nigh unto the city, Peter went up upon the housetop to pray about the sixth hour:

10 And he became very hungry, and would have eaten: but while they made ready, he fell into a trance,

11 And saw heaven opened, and a certain vessel descending unto him, as it had been a great sheet knit at the four corners, and let down to the earth.

God showed Peter through a vision that He was going to bring in the Gentiles. Now we will skip to verse 19:

ACTS 10:19–20

19 While Peter thought on the vision, THE SPIRIT SAID unto him, Behold, three men seek thee.

20 Arise therefore, and get thee down, and go with them, doubting nothing: for I have sent them.

These were three men from Cornelius' household. After Peter went to Cornelius' house in Caesarea and preached to these Gentiles, he went up to Jerusalem where the Bible says, "... *they that were of the circumcision contended with him*" (Acts 11:2). In Acts chapter 11, Peter is rehearsing what had happened to him in Acts chapter 10.

ACTS 11:11–12

11 And, behold, immediately there were three men already come unto the house where I was, sent from Caesarea unto me.

12 AND THE SPIRIT BADE ME GO with them, nothing doubting . . . .

The Holy Spirit spoke to Peter. It may have been that Peter looked around to see who had spoken to him, I don't know. But he knew that the Spirit of God bade him go.

The Spirit spoke to me as I was waiting there in my church. The Holy Spirit said, "I am going to take you on to revelations and visions."

Immediately, revelations, in line with the Word—I'm not talking about something out of line with the Bible—began to come. Then in 1950 the visions began to come. Jesus Himself appeared to me and talked to me on various occasions. There were also other visions.

CHAPTER 24

The Spirit Bade Me Go

Now there were in the church that was at Antioch
certain prophets and teachers;
as Barnabas, and Simeon that was called Niger,
and Lucius of Cyrene, and Manaen,
which had been brought up with Herod the tetrarch, and Saul.
As they ministered to the Lord, and fasted,
THE HOLY GHOST SAID,
Separate me Barnabas and Saul for the work
whereunto I have called them.

—Acts 13:1–2

T he Holy Ghost *said*. It would be of interest, first of all, to notice under what   conditions the Holy Ghost said something. *"As they ministered to the Lord, and fasted, the Holy Ghost said. . . ."*

I am convinced we need to have services where we minister to the Lord. Too often we just minister to one another. Bible studies are good; we need them. Special singing is fine. But too many times we are not singing to the Lord; we are singing to the congregation. Let's have some services where we minister to the Lord; where we wait on Him. In that kind of an atmosphere the Holy Ghost can speak to us.

This was a group of five ministers. I do not know how the Holy Ghost spoke to them. It could have been that one of the prophets spoke it out. Of this I am sure—they all heard and they all agreed that the Holy Ghost was talking.

The Holy Ghost said, *"Separate me Barnabas and Saul for the work whereunto I have called them"* (Acts 13:2).

Peter said, *". . . The Spirit bade me go. . . "* (Acts 11:12). After I had been in the ministry many years, death came and fastened itself upon my body. I know when death comes, I have been dead twice and came back. I know how it feels. Actually, I started to fall into the arms of death, when the Spirit of God came on me and lifted me up.

I heard a Voice speak. To me it was audible. I believe it was Jesus. I know that it was the Holy Spirit speaking. We discussed earlier how the Holy Ghost speaks not of Himself, but whatever He hears, that shall He speak. So the Holy Spirit heard God or Jesus say this, and He repeated it.

It sounded like a man's voice. It said, "Thou shalt not die, but thou shalt live. I want you to go teach My people faith. I have taught you faith through My Word. I have permitted you to go through certain experiences. You have learned faith both through My Word and by experience. Now go teach My people what I have taught you. Go teach My people faith."

The moment that voice ceased speaking I was perfectly well.

I have endeavored to be obedient to that heavenly Voice. That is the reason I teach faith so much—I am supposed to do it.

I will refer again now to the time Jesus appeared to me in 1959 in El Paso, Texas. It was during this vision that He told me, "Go teach My people how to be led by My Spirit." I have been dilatory about this. But I am going to do more teaching on this from now on. This is the reason for this book.

CHAPTER *25*

Guidance Through Prophecy

Follow after charity, and desire spiritual gifts,
but rather that ye may prophesy.

—1 Corinthians 14:1

Are all apostles? are all prophets? are all teachers?
are all workers of miracles?

—1 Corinthians 12:29

Paul, speaking to the elders of the church at Ephesus in his farewell message, said, *"And now, behold, I go bound in the spirit unto Jerusalem, not knowing the things that shall befall me there: Save that the Holy Ghost witnesseth in every city, saying that bonds and afflictions abide me"* (Acts 20:22–23).

Then in chapter 21, while on his journey Paul landed at Tyre where the ship was to be unladen. Luke, the writer of Acts, was with Paul. He wrote, *"And finding disciples, we tarried there seven days: who said to Paul through the Spirit, that he should not go up to Jerusalem"* (v. 4).

Paul continued on his journey:

ACTS 21:8–14

8 And the next day we that were of Paul's company departed, and came unto Caesarea: and we entered into the house of Philip the evangelist, which was one of the seven; and abode with him.

9 And the same man had four daughters, virgins, which did prophesy.

10 And as we tarried there many days, there came down from Judaea a certain prophet, named Agabus.

11 And when he was come unto us, he took Paul's girdle, and bound his own hands and feet, and said, Thus saith the Holy Ghost, So shall the Jews at Jerusalem bind the man that owneth this girdle, and shall deliver him into the hands of the Gentiles.

12 And when we heard these things, both we, and they of that place, besought him not to go up to Jerusalem.

13 Then Paul answered, What mean ye to weep and to break mine heart? for I am ready not to be bound only, but also to die at Jerusalem for the name of the Lord Jesus.

14 And when he would not be persuaded, we ceased, saying, The will of the Lord be done.

Some have thought that Paul missed it. However, when Paul did go up to Jerusalem and was arrested, Jesus stood by Paul in the night.

He appeared to him in a vision. He did not rebuke Paul. Jesus did not tell Paul that he had missed it. He said, *". . . Be of good cheer, Paul: for as thou hast testified of me in Jerusalem, so must thou bear witness also at Rome"* (Acts 23:11).

No, Paul did not miss it. What God was doing was preparing Paul for what was ahead of him.

Notice that we have two different things operating here: (1) the gift of prophecy; (2) the ministry of the prophet. They are different. They are not the same. It is a mistake to confuse the two, yet this is often done.

The fact that one prophesies does not make him a prophet. The Word of God plainly teaches that everyone should desire to prophesy (1 Cor. 14:1). However, if just *prophesying* made you a prophet, then it would seem that the Lord was saying that everyone should desire to be a *prophet*. Yet Paul asked, *"Are all apostles? are all prophets?. . ."* (1 Cor. 12:29). The answer is no. Since all could not be prophets, God would not tell us to seek something we could not have.

The simple gift of prophecy is speaking unto men to edification and exhortation and comfort (1 Cor. 14:3). Prophecy is a supernatural utterance in a known tongue—your own tongue. (Speaking in tongues is supernatural utterance in an unknown tongue—a tongue unknown to you.) Prophecy can be used in prayer, as well as tongues.

Sometimes when you are prophesying, it seems as if there are two of you. It seems to me as if I am standing right beside myself. You see, it is coming from my inward man where the Spirit of God Who is prophesying abides. I listen with my natural ears to see what He said.

The Office of the Prophet

There is the office of the prophet. Without going into detail about it, we will touch the office of the prophet briefly concerning guidance. For one to be a prophet, he stands in that office and uses that ministry. Other spiritual gifts besides prophecy must operate in his ministry. The simple gift of prophecy, as we have said, is for speaking unto men for edification, and exhortation, and comfort. In this simple gift of prophecy there is no *foretelling*—no prediction whatsoever. However, in the ministry of the prophet there is foretelling and prediction. A prophet has the revelation gifts (the word of wisdom, the word of knowledge, and/or the discerning of spirits) in operation along with prophecy.

It is important to realize that spiritual things can be misused just as natural things can be misused. Some folks have never realized that. They think that just because it is spiritual, it has to be perfect—that it cannot be misused.

I have known people who were at one time wealthy who are now bankrupt because they listened to someone prophesy how to invest their money.

I remember a dear man who was in one of my meetings. I knew who he was, but I didn't really know him. I did not know that he would never make a business deal without calling a so-called "prophet" to prophesy to him what to do.

I said to him, "I seem to be impressed to say this to you. You are going to lose everything you have and go bankrupt if you keep listening to whoever is advising you."

He didn't listen. The poor fellow, who was very wealthy, lost his home and everything he had. I have seen this happen not just one time, but many times.

I have seen ministers who have lost their ministries because of wrong prophecies.

You have to judge prophecies by the Word of God. If prophecy is not in line with the Word of God, it is not right.

Secondly, you have to judge personal prophecies by what you have in your own spirit. If you do not have something in your own spirit, do not accept a personal prophecy.

For years I have traveled extensively in the ministry. Everywhere I go there is always someone who has a "word" from the Lord for me—sometimes two or three. In all these years only one or two of them have been correct.

Do not build your life on prophecies. Do not guide your life by prophecies. Build your life on the Word! Let those other things be secondary. Put the Word of God first!

People sometimes say, "Well, if God is doing it, it has to be all right."

You have to realize that it isn't exactly God doing it. It is men prophesying under the inspiration of the Spirit of God. Anything that man has to do with is not perfect. The Spirit of God is perfect. The gifts of the Spirit in themselves are perfect. But they certainly are not always perfect in manifestation, because they are manifested through imperfect vessels. This is the reason prophecy and tongues with interpretation need to be judged by the Word.

1 CORINTHIANS 14:29–30

29 Let the prophets speak two or three, and let the other judge.

30 If any thing be revealed to another that sitteth by, let the first hold his peace.

"Let the prophets speak. . . ." The Bible is talking about prophets here—not just anyone who prophesies. Do not accept something just because a prophet said it. It is to be judged according to the Bible. We do not judge people. We judge what was said.

Now notice verse 30. *"If any thing be revealed to another* [prophet]. . . ."
Prophets have revelations. Others might occasionally, but prophets have
a ministry along this line.

1 CORINTHIANS 14:32

32 And the spirits of the prophets are subject to the
prophets.

Some have said, "God made me do that. I couldn't help but say
that." The spirits of the prophets are subject to the prophets. That
means a person does not have to say it. It comes out of his spirit. It
is subject to him. The gift of tongues, the interpretation of tongues,
and prophecy operate under the unction of the Spirit. And it might
be that God through these methods would give us a word of knowledge, a word of wisdom, or revelation as we need it. But we initiate
the operation of prophecy. We initiate the operation of tongues and
interpretation. We are the ones who have to speak it out.

Many times when the Spirit of God is moving, anyone who can
prophesy could do so—but that does not mean one should. Also,
when the Spirit is in manifestation, anyone who is used in the ministry gift of tongues and interpretation could speak—but that does not
mean he should. Have that unction of the Spirit to do it—otherwise
just sit there and let God move through someone else who has it.

I held a seven-week meeting in a church years ago. Every single
night about the same time, at the same spot in the service, just as they
got ready to pass the offering plates, this woman got up and spoke
with tongues. She said the same thing in tongues every night. After a
while I could have said the same things she said. If no one else would
interpret it, she would. It was like someone poured cold water over
the crowd. It deadened the service.

The pastor asked me to teach the auditorium class one Sunday morning when he had to be out of town. This was unusual—but I finished before the bell rang. One of the deacons said, "Brother Hagin, may I ask a question?"

"Well, yes," I said. I thought it would be in line with the lesson.

He said, "When messages in tongues with interpretation are given in public assembly, shouldn't they be a blessing to the congregation? Should it kill the service?"

That dear woman was sitting right in front of me.

I said, "That is beside the lesson. I'd rather not get into that right now."

But others, some of the leaders of the church, said, "Brother Hagin, we ought to answer that."

So I said, "If it is in the Spirit, it will lift the service high. It will not push it down."

That woman was intelligent enough to catch on to that. She came to me and said, "I have been wrong, haven't I?"

I said, "Yes ma'am, you have."

She said, "I thought so all the time. There was a witness on the inside of me that knew that. But I wanted to be used of God. I am going to stop that."

I said, "Thank you. You are a real blessing to the church."

Others might have gotten angry about it saying, "They won't allow God to move."

Sometimes folks do speak out, like this woman, without the unction of the Spirit. This does not do away with the fact that her tongues were real. However, they were in imperfect operation. They were misused.

I admonish people to be very careful about personal prophecies. So many lives have been shipwrecked and ruined by not being careful regarding personal prophecy. Don't marry someone because someone prophesied you should. I have seen many such so-called "prophecies" through the years. I have never seen one of those marriages work out yet. Homes have been broken up by so-called prophecies.

Also, don't go into the ministry because somebody prophesied you should. Get it on the inside of you for yourself. Then if a prophecy confirms what you already have, that's all right. Jesus said to me when He appeared in that vision in 1959, "If the prophecy confirms what you already have, accept it. If it does not, don't accept it."

The Holy Ghost said, "Separate me Barnabas and Saul for the work whereunto I have called them" (Acts 13:2). He had already called them. This was just a confirmation of it.

In the last church I pastored there was a certain young person who was beautiful spiritually. My wife said to me, "I believe the hand of the Lord is on him. God is calling him into the ministry."

I said, "I have that conviction myself. But I am not going to "call" anyone. I am not going to tell anyone they are called, even if I know they are."

This is why. When one gets out in the ministry, it isn't always easy. Paul told the young minister, Timothy, "Endure hardness as a good soldier" (2 Tim. 2:3). When the way gets hard—and it will—you can have the victory. But it will get hard and someone who is not convinced of the call for themselves may say, "I just went because Daddy said so." Or, "Someone prophesied to me; I really don't know that I am called." But one who makes that dedication from his own spirit, who knows God called him, will stand through hell or high water.

So I did not say anything to this young person. Then one Sunday night we were all praying around the altar. I went around and laid hands on people to pray as God would lead me. I stopped beside this young man who was kneeling in the altar in intense prayer. I opened my mouth to pray, but I heard these words come out, "This is a confirmation of what I said to you at 3 o'clock this afternoon as you were praying down in the storm cellar. You asked for a confirmation and this is it. That was Me speaking to you."

After the prayer service I asked, "Were you praying down in the storm cellar at 3 o'clock this afternoon?"

(I wanted to check up—if I am wrong, I want to get right. If I miss it, I just admit, "I missed it." Don't be afraid to say, "I missed it." When I first started learning to drive a car I missed it a few times and ran up over the curb. But I didn't quit driving just because I missed it. Did you? We ought to have as much sense about spiritual things. Just because I missed it, I am not going to quit. I am going to keep going. I will just see to it that I don't miss it again. So I was checking up on it to see.)

This young person said, "Yes, I was praying. You know, Brother Hagin, I have felt for some time that God had a call on my life, but I didn't say yes or no. So I was spending time down in the cellar (which was fixed up like a nice basement) praying, meditating, reading the Bible, waiting on God. I felt that the Lord spoke to me and said, 'I have called you to the ministry—and I will confirm it tonight in the service.' But I didn't know how He would."

Remember—if it does not bear witness, or confirm something you already have, do not accept a personal prophecy.

As long as the gift of prophecy stays in the realm of speaking to men for edification, exhortation, and comfort, it is wonderful. Encourage that. But many times someone who prophesies may see a prophet minister with a word of foreknowledge. Then he begins to think, "I prophesy, so I can do that." Then he moves out of the place where he should be, into the other realm where he should not be.

A woman came up to me in one of our seminars we held in Tulsa. She had come with a group from a nearby city. She said, "Brother Hagin, this is all new to us. In our town we have a weekly prayer group. I want to ask you something about it. Some of them think I am wrong, but I don't think what we are doing is right. Actually, I don't know if I would call it a prayer meeting—all they ever do is lay hands on one another and prophesy. They spend all afternoon prophesying over one another. And I don't ever get anything but a bad prophecy.

"They prophesied that my mother was going to die within six months. That was 18 months ago and she is not dead. Then they prophesied that my husband was going to leave me. He's not saved but he is a fine man and I love him. He is a good provider. We don't have any trouble. Those are just two examples. I always get prophecies that something bad is going to happen—but nothing bad has ever happened."

I said, "No, and it won't either. You are a child of God."

She said, "Isn't that a misuse?"

I said, "Yes, it is."

We need to know these things. It is very easy for babies to be mis-led and misguided. We can get off track. That's why Paul wrote to the church at Corinth about these things.

CHAPTER 26

Guidance Through Visions

There was a certain man in Caesarea called Cornelius,
a centurion of the band called the Italian band,
A devout man, and one that feared God with all his house,
which gave much alms to the people, and prayed to God alway.
He saw in a vision evidently about the ninth hour of the day
an angel of God coming in to him, and saying unto him. . . .

—Acts 10:1–3

Sometimes God leads through visions.

Cornelius was a devout man, but he was not born again. He did not know about Jesus. He was a Jewish proselyte. The angel who appeared to him in this vision could not preach the gospel to him.

God did not call angels to preach the gospel; God called men to preach the Gospel. However, the angel did tell Cornelius where to send for someone who could preach the Gospel to him and tell him how to be saved.

Cornelius saw an angel in a vision. Angels also have the ability, as God permits, to take upon themselves a visible form which can be seen with the natural eye, just as you can see a physical person.

HEBREWS 13:2

2 Be not forgetful to entertain strangers: for thereby some have entertained angels unawares.

The scripture calls Cornelius' experience a vision (Acts 10:3). It was a spiritual vision. Cornelius saw into the spirit world, and there are angels out there in the spirit world. If others had been present, they would not have seen anything. Yet if the angel had taken on a visible form, anyone could have seen it.

There are three kinds of visions: spiritual visions, trances, and open visions.

In a spiritual vision, you see with the eyes of your spirit—not with your physical eye. When Paul saw the Lord in Acts chapter 9, it was a spiritual vision. He did not see Him with his physical eyes.

ACTS 9:8

8 And Saul arose from the earth; and when his eyes were opened, he saw no man: but they led him by the hand, and brought him into Damascus.

When the Lord spoke to Saul, his eyes were shut. Therefore, whatever it was that Paul saw, he did not see it with his physical eyes. We know this because the Bible says that when his eyes WERE OPENED, he was blind.

The second type of vision is when one falls into a trance. Cornelius did not fall into a trance—but Peter did.

ACTS 10:9–11

9 On the morrow, as they went on their journey, and drew nigh unto the city, Peter went up upon the housetop to pray about the sixth hour:

10 And he became very hungry, and would have eaten: but while they made ready, he fell into a trance,

11 And saw heaven opened, and a certain vessel descending unto him, as it had been a great sheet knit at the four corners, and let down to the earth.

When one falls into a trance, his physical senses are suspended. He does not know where he is right at the moment. He is not unconscious, but he does not know what is going on around him. He is more conscious of spiritual things than physical things.

The third type of vision is what I call an open vision. The vision that occurred in El Paso in 1959 (which I have referred to in this book), was an open vision. My eyes were wide open. My physical senses were intact. I did not fall into a trance. Jesus walked into my room. I saw Him with my physical eyes.

Of all the visions I have had, only two were open visions. Three of them occurred when I fell into a trance. The rest were spiritual visions.

There were different types of visions in the Acts of the Apostles. There are different types of visions now.

For example, in visions, sometimes things are symbolic. In Peter's vision they were. He saw all manner of creeping things, both clean and unclean. He had to think on the vision in order to understand it (Acts 10:19). The Spirit spoke to him as he thought upon the vision and bade him go with three men to Cornelius' house. Peter still didn't know exactly what the vision meant. But when he went, things happened, and he began to understand that God had called the Gentiles into redemption as well as the Jews.

ACTS 8:26–29

26 And the angel of the Lord spake unto Philip, saying, Arise, and go toward the south unto the way that goeth down from Jerusalem unto Gaza, which is desert.

27 And he arose and went: and, behold, a man of Ethiopia, an eunuch of great authority under Candace queen of the Ethiopians, who had the charge of all her treasure, and had come to Jerusalem for to worship,

28 Was returning, and sitting in his chariot read Esaias the prophet.

29 Then the Spirit said unto Philip, Go near, and join thyself to this chariot.

Some church people admit that God spoke to the apostles such as Peter, but they say that such divine visitations were only for the apostles. But Philip was not an apostle. He was elected as a deacon first (Acts 6:5). The highest office he ever filled was that of the evangelist (Acts 21:8). Isn't it sad that in the church world we have been robbed of the blessings and the supernatural manifestations we should have had because people closed the book on the supernatural and said, "That was just for the apostles. All that ceased when the apostles of the New Testament died."

ACTS 9:10–12

10 And there was a certain disciple at Damascus, named Ananias; and to him said the Lord in a vision, Ananias. And he said, Behold, I am here, Lord.

11 And the Lord said unto him, Arise, and go into the street which is called Straight, and enquire in the house of Judas for one called Saul of Tarsus: for, behold, he prayeth,

12 And hath seen in a vision a man named Ananias coming in, and putting his hand on him, that he might receive his sight.

Ananias was not a deacon. He was just a disciple. He was what we would call a layman. Yet the Lord used him. We should all put ourselves in a position where God can use us as He sees fit. We don't have to wait for a vision before we do something for God. God may give us a vision, or He may not. An angel may appear to us, or one may not.

It was a great privilege for me to speak in the church of a certain great man of God when he was past seventy years of age. He had been filled with the Spirit way back at the turn of the century and had gone out to China as a missionary in 1912. He told me of many marvelous experiences he'd had.

He had a Bible study every Friday night in his church. (I believe he was one of the world's foremost Bible teachers—and I have heard most of them.) He related this to me: He said he would teach certain subjects as the Lord directed, but he also let the congregation suggest subjects by writing them down on a slip of paper. On one occasion, the majority of the congregation wrote, "We would like some teaching on angels. We have never heard any teaching on that subject."

He had spent a number of years teaching in one of the best Pentecostal Bible schools, and he thought he could cover the subject in two weeks. But he said, "The more I studied, the bigger it got. I taught six weeks and still did not cover the subject."

This man was an official of his Full Gospel denomination. Soon after this teaching on angels he was in a business meeting with leaders of that denomination. One matter of discussion concerned the report that a minister of their denomination claimed to have seen an angel. He said that the angel instructed him concerning his ministry. They were about to bar him from the denomination.

This Bible teacher said, "I just sat there and listened. I didn't even comment. I never did talk unless I was called on to talk. I could see the trend; they were about ready to turn this other minister out of the denomination."

Finally, one brother got up and said, "I believe we ought to hear from Brother S. He has been with us from the beginning of the movement. He is one of our most able Bible teachers. Let's hear what he has to say."

He told me he began by telling them about the study of angels he had just completed and taught in his church. Then he said, "I am not the least bit concerned because one out of several thousand of our ministers has seen an angel. The thing that disturbs me is why more of us are not seeing them.

"Then secondly," he told them, "if we are going to turn this man out for seeing an angel who instructed him concerning his ministry, what are we going to give our people in the place of it? Do we have anything better? anything more supernatural? anything more scriptural? If we do not, I think we had better stay with what we have."

Quickly, someone jumped to his feet and said, "I move that we table this and forget all about it." They voted unanimously to leave it alone.

In 1963, my office occupied only the den of my little frame home in Garland, Texas. It wasn't really much of an office at that. Some men in another city contacted me. They said, "If you will move your office to this city, we will set up an office for you. We will buy all the office equipment, hire the secretaries, and pay their salaries. You won't have to pay anything. Let's get some of your material published."

Another man, who was an electronic technician, said, "Brother Hagin, if you will let me, I will make tapes of all your sermons. It won't cost you a thing. I will furnish all the materials free of charge."

Those offers sounded good. You would think God must be in them. But about that time I was praying with a certain group. We were having special times of ministering to the Lord. It was the kind of atmosphere Acts 13:1 and 2 speaks of—an atmosphere where God will move.

I was sitting on the platform beside a chair, praying, when suddenly Jesus stood right in front of me. I had my eyes shut. It was a spiritual vision. I did not fall into a trance. Standing right behind Jesus, about two feet to His right and three feet behind Him, was a large angel. I had seen angels before—but never one that big. He must have been 8 feet tall or more.

Jesus talked to me about some things. (And everything He said came to pass.) Occasionally, while He talked, I would glance at that angel. When I did, the angel would open his mouth and start to say something. When I looked back to Jesus, he would not say anything.

After Jesus finished His conversation with me, I asked, "Who is that fellow? What does he represent?"

Jesus said, "That's your angel."

I said, "My angel?"

"Yes," He said, "your angel. You read in the Scriptures that I said concerning the little children that their angel is ever before My Father's face. You don't lose your angel just because you grow up."

(Isn't that comforting! I have that big fellow following me around. Praise the Lord!)

I said, "What does he want?"

Jesus said, "He has a message for you."

Then I got so letter-of-the-Word conscious I could have missed the Spirit. I said, "You are talking to me; why don't You give me the message? Why do I have to listen to an angel? Besides that, the Word of God says as many as are led by the Spirit of God, they are the sons of God. I have the Holy Ghost. Why couldn't the Holy Ghost talk to me?"

Jesus had mercy on me, and patience with me. He said, "Did you ever read in My Word where the angel of the Lord told Philip to go down to the way of Gaza? Wasn't that direction? Wasn't that guidance? Didn't my angel appear to Cornelius, and he wasn't even a born-again man? Didn't the angel tell him what to do?"

He gave me several more New Testament examples. Finally, I said, "That's enough. I will listen." Then I looked up to this big fellow and said, "What is it?"

He started this way, "I am sent from the Presence of Almighty God to tell you not to let these men (and he called their names) set up an office for you. They have an ulterior motive. They will control your ministry because they will have put in all the money."

Then he called the name of the man who was the radio and electronic technician and said, "Don't let him have any of your tapes. He has an ulterior motive. If he gets them into his hands, he will control them. I am sent from the Presence of Almighty God to tell you that.

"Then I am sent from the Presence of Almighty God to tell you this: The money will come so that you can set up your own office, have your own books, have your own tapes. You will be the head of it, the sole boss, because I am going to tell you what to do, and not some man. Within four months, after everything is paid and cleared out, you will have enough money to get you headed this direction. For I have sent my angels out to cause the money to come."

When that time came, I had $4,000 which was enough to do what the Lord had told me to do. That was the beginning of this ministry.

I could tell more, but this is enough to illustrate that these things do happen. But let me emphasize this—although God does lead us through visions and other supernatural manifestations, I would encourage you NOT to seek a vision. You could get beyond the Word where the devil can deceive you. We often prefer to have a more direct word of guidance, but we don't always have it. So don't try to manufacture it, if it is not there. Nowhere in the Bible does it say that anyone was seeking a vision when one came. Visions just happened without anyone in the Bible seeking them.

Be content, if it is all you ever have, to follow the inward witness. But educate and train and develop your human spirit so that inward witness becomes more and more real to you.

Then, if God sees fit for supernatural visitations and manifestations, just thank God for them.

Know that the angels of God are with you. Your angel is with you whether you ever see him or not.

CHAPTER 27

Listen to Your Heart

Now when much time was spent,
and when sailing was now dangerous, because the fast was now already past,
Paul admonished them, And said unto them,
Sirs, I PERCEIVE that this voyage will be with hurt and much damage,
not only of the lading and ship, but also of our lives.

—Acts 27:9–10

Paul did not say, "The Lord told me" that this voyage will be with much hurt and damage. He simply said, "I *perceive*" that it will. In his spirit, Paul had an inward perception, an inward premonition, an inward witness that the voyage would be dangerous. This is the primary way God leads all of us.

Paul did not perceive it *mentally*. He did not have some kind of "vibration" or psychic experience. I don't like this "vibration" business. Spiritual perceptions are not in the psychic realm. You do not find psychic phenomenon in the Bible. Also, Paul did not perceive this *physically*. In his *spirit* he had a witness.

That belongs to all of us. The Holy Spirit abiding in our spirits must communicate with us through our spirits—not through our minds. That is why your spirit knows things your head doesn't know. But we have not been taught to listen to our spirits. And sometimes we are reluctant to do so.

The reason that we as Spirit-filled believers continually miss it, make mistakes, and fail is because our spirits, which should guide us, are kept locked away in prison, so to speak. Knowledge, or intellect, has taken the throne.

Any person who shuts his spirit away and never listens to it—because the spirit of man is the candle of the Lord—becomes crippled in life and becomes an easy prey to selfish and designing people.

My wife and I held a meeting for a certain lady pastor—a very spiritually beautiful woman—who related this story to me herself:

An evangelist was coming to town. He got all the churches he could to cooperate with him in a citywide meeting. He rented the city auditorium. It is a sorry thing to have to say, but everyone in the ministry is not honest. Because this man had a poor credit rating, the city auditorium demanded payment in advance. So he went through this woman pastor. She was gullible enough to say her church would stand responsible for $3,000 rent and all newspaper advertising. Crowds of 2,000 to 3,000 attended every night. He took up a lot of money, but he left town without paying one bill. This woman's church had to take $5,000 out of their building fund to cover this evangelist's expenses.

This lady pastor told me, "Brother Hagin, if I had listened to my heart, I would never have done that."

I said to her, "I heard you recovered your money."

She said, "I sure did. I found out where he was holding a meeting in another state. I got an airplane ticket and went there. The service had already started. I waited. Just when they were about to turn the service to him I marched down the aisle and toward the platform. An usher tried to stop me. I said, 'No, I am a minister of the Gospel. I want to see this scoundrel.' I walked right up on the platform and plopped myself down beside him.

"I said, 'I have come after my $5,000. I will take the offering tonight. I brought my attaché case along. We will dump all the offering in there. And I will stay around here every night until my church recovers all of our money.'

"He said, 'Well, now we . . .'

"I said, 'No, if you don't give me back all of my money, when they say they are going to turn the service over to you, I am going to take the pulpit and tell the people what happened. And not only that, I am going to follow you from meeting to meeting. In every meeting, I am going to come up on the platform and make the same announcement and tell the people what you did.'"

Needless to say, in two nights she had her money and she was on her way home. I glory in her spunk.

But the point I want to make is this. She said to me, "Brother Hagin, if I had listened to my spirit, this never would have happened. I don't mean if I had listened to a voice; I don't even mean a still, small voice. I just mean if I had listened to the inward witness. I had a check in my spirit. If I had listened to it, I wouldn't have stood good for his debts."

If we as individuals would have listened to our hearts—to an inward witness, or an inward voice—we would not have done some things we did.

I have lost money by not listening to that inward witness. I knew on the inside that I should not do some things. Why did I do it? Well, why do any of us not listen to the inward witness?

But just because you make a mistake, don't quit. You don't quit physically just because you make a mistake. If the phone rings in the middle of the night and you stumble over a stool and fall down trying to answer it, you don't just lie there. You get up and answer the phone. Just because you bust your shins or stub your toe physically, you don't quit. And just because you bust your shins or stub your toe spiritually, you don't quit either.

As I said, the person who keeps his spirit shut away and never listens to it becomes crippled in life. The person who listens to his spirit is the man or woman, boy or girl who climbs to the top!

If Christians would just check up on the inside of them in most of the affairs of life, they would know what to do.

You do not need to seek guidance when the Bible has already told you what to do. Go ahead and do it. The Bible tells you how to act in every circumstance of life. It tells husbands how to treat wives. It tells wives how to treat husbands. It tells parents how to treat their children. It tells children how to respond to their parents. The Bible tells all of us to walk in love—divine love. And that divine love, which seeks not its own, is also a matter of the heart.

CHAPTER *28*

How to Train the Human Spirit

The spirit of man is the candle of the Lord. . . .

—Proverbs 20:27

The Lord enlightens us and guides us through our spirits. If that be the case—and it is—then we need to become more spirit-conscious. We need to become more conscious of the fact that we are spirit beings, and not just mental or physical beings. We need to train our spirits so they will become safer and safer guides.

One thing which has held back the Christian world as a whole is that we are more physical-conscious (body-conscious) and more mental-conscious (soul-conscious) than we are spirit-conscious. We have developed the body and the soul, but we have left the spirit of man almost untouched. Wow!

I have a cassette teaching tape which has helped many Christians in this area. In one of our meetings, one young man I know quite well gave his testimony of how it had helped him:

Just a few years ago, when he was 31 or 32, he went into business. He left his salaried job with a total of $5,500. He was single at that time and he had to use this money for living expenses as well as for capital. At one point, his nest egg dwindled to $50.

He gave this testimony: "I listened to Brother Hagin's tapes. There were three on faith and confession, and one called "How to Train the Human Spirit." I went to bed every night listening to that tape. I put it on in the morning and listened to it while I shaved. I listened to it over and over and over again—probably hundreds of times—until that message got into my spirit. Then by listening to my spirit and using my faith, my assets now total in excess of $30 million."

This young man is only about 38 years old now. He is not a preacher. He is a businessman. He has told me how his spirit has spoken to him and told him how to invest and buy land.

I will give the essence of the teaching contained on that cassette in this chapter: How to Train the Human Spirit.

Your spirit can be educated just as your mind can be educated. Your spirit can be built up in strength and trained just as your body can be built and trained. Here are four rules by which you can train and develop your own human spirit.

1. By meditation in the Word
2. By practicing the Word
3. By giving the Word first place
4. By instantly obeying the voice of your spirit

By Meditation in the Word of God

The most deeply spiritual men and women I know are those who give time to meditation in the Word of God. You cannot develop spiritual wisdom without meditation. God made that fact known to Joshua just after the death of Moses at the very beginning of Joshua's ministry.

JOSHUA 1:8

8 This book of the law shall not depart out of thy mouth; but thou shalt meditate therein day and night, that thou mayest observe to do according to all that is written therein: for then thou shalt make thy way prosperous, and then thou shalt have good success.

If God did not want Joshua to be prosperous, why did He tell him how to prosper? If He did not want him to succeed, why did He tell him how to have good success? He wanted Joshua to be successful—and He wants you to be successful. Yes & Amen.

Paraphrasing this truth in New Testament language, we would say, "The Word of God—particularly the New Testament—shall not depart out of your mouth. But meditate therein day and night, that you may observe to do according to all that is written therein: for then you will make your way prosperous and you will have good success."

If you ever want to do anything great in life, if you ever want to amount to anything in life, *take time to meditate in the Word of God.* Start out with at least 10 or 15 minutes a day—then increase the time.

I left the last church I pastored in 1949 and I have been out in the field ministry ever since. I used to do much more fasting and a different kind of praying than I do now. (You learn things as you go along.)

Running two services a day—which I always did—and sometimes three, takes a lot out of you physically as well as spiritually. I would teach every morning, pray out loud all afternoon, and preach every night. I ate only one meal a day during my meetings and by exerting so much physical energy, I would grow weak. Then two days a week were my fast days—Tuesday and Thursday. I ate no food and drank no water for 24 hours.

One day the Lord said to me, "I would rather you would live a fasted life instead of having days and periods of fasting."

I said, "What do you mean? I never heard anyone say that!"

The Lord said, "Instead of having certain days you fast and then going back and eating all you want, just live a fasted life. Fasting does not change Me anyhow. I am the same before you fast, while you fast, and when you get through fasting. It does not change My Word. It helps you keep your flesh under. So just don't ever eat all you want. Just keep your flesh under all the time."

Then He said, "Don't spend all that time in the afternoon praying and wearing yourself out before the night service. Lie on the bed and meditate."

So I began to lie there in the afternoons, meditating. And I got further meditating than I ever did praying and fasting. I grew more spiritually.

That is what God is saying in Joshua 1:8: ". . . for then thou shalt make thy way prosperous . . ." I wanted to be prosperous in the ministry. "and then thou shalt have good success." I wanted to have good success in the ministry. This works whether you are in the ministry, whether you raise cattle, sell automobiles, or whatever you do.

This Word of God shall not depart out of thy mouth. Talk about the Word. But thou shalt meditate therein. Think on the Word.

The Hebrew word translated meditate, also carries this thought with it: To mutter. Mutter the Word. Speak it to yourself.

The Lord led me, before I ever heard anyone teach on meditation, to lie on the bed and mutter the Word. I just said it to myself. And I would have some of the most tremendous services. I developed myself spiritually, and at the same time conserved my physical strength.

I like another translation of Joshua 1:8. The last phrase reads like this: ". . . you shall be able to deal wisely in the affairs of life." You could not have good success if you did not know how to deal wisely in the affairs of life.

How can you know how to deal wisely in the affairs of life? Because you meditated in the Word of God and walked in the light of that Word.

Practicing the Word

Practicing the Word means being a doer of the Word.

JAMES 1:22

22 But be ye doers of the word, and not hearers only . . . .

We have many "talkers about the Word," and even many "rejoicers about the Word," but we do not have many "doers of the Word."

Begin to practice being a doer of the Word by doing in all circumstances what the Word tells you to do.

Some have thought that being a doer of the Word meant to keep the Ten Commandments. That is not what James 1:22 means. After all, under the New Covenant we have but one commandment—the commandment of love. Jesus said, *"A new commandment I give unto you, That ye love one another; as I have loved you, that ye also love one another"* (John 13:34).

139

A doer of the Word will do that. If you love someone, you won't steal from him. You won't lie about him. The New Testament says that love is the fulfilling of the law. If you walk in love you won't break any law that was given to curb sin.

Being a doer of the Word means that we are to do primarily what is written in the Epistles. They are the letters written to us, the Church. As an example of doing the Word, let us look at some instructions given us in one of the Epistles.

PHILIPPIANS 4:6

6 Be careful for nothing; but in every thing by prayer and supplication with thanksgiving let your requests be made known unto God.

So do that! Now we don't mind practicing part of this verse—the part that says to pray. But if you practice just that part and not the first part, you are not practicing the Word—you are not a doer of the Word.

The Amplified translation of Philippians 4:6 begins, "Do not fret or have any anxiety about anything. . . ." First we are told not to fret. If you are going to fret and have anxieties, it will do no good to make requests. That kind of praying does not work. An over-anxious prayer full of fretfulness does not work.

I felt very sorry for a minister who came to me some years ago. (But sometimes it doesn't give a man the answer just to sympathize with him.) His life was full of storms and tests. His stomach was upset; he couldn't keep down what he ate. He couldn't sleep. His nerves were shot because of a particular incident.

He came to me for help. I began to tell him what the Word said and how to pray about this circumstance. When I encouraged him to

take this scripture and *do it*, he rebelled. He said, "Oh
one doesn't have the faith that you have."

I told him it was not a matter of having a lot of faith, but a matter
of endeavoring to practice the Word. I told him if he would practice
the Word, his faith would be built up. And I told him how I practice
this particular verse.

When I get alone, I read this verse aloud and I tell the Lord that
His Word is true and that I believe it.

I told this minister that he would be tempted to say he couldn't
help worrying and fretting. But that God had not asked us to do
something we cannot do. When God said not to fret—that means we
can keep from fretting and being anxious. God is a just God and He
will not ask us to do something we cannot do.

When I first began practicing this verse it was easy to believe that
I could make my requests known unto God—but it was hard to
believe that I could *not fret*. However, since God says we don't have
to fret, then I would say, "I refuse to fret or have any anxiety about
anything."

I tell the Lord that I bring my requests unto Him. Then I thank
Him for the answer. This quiets my spirit and pacifies the troubled
spirit the devil tries to make me have.

Then I would go about my business. Before I knew it, however, the
devil was trying to get me to fret again. I would simply go right back
and read this verse again and keep claiming it.

This minister began to practice Philippians 4:6. He told me later
that the problem worked out and did not get as big as he was expecting. He was about to be sued over a certain matter, but God helped
him out of it.

It is possible to become so fretful over something that you cannot
eat or sleep. But all you have to do is practice the Word and you will
get results.

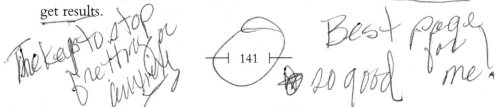

Philippians 4:7 is a result of practicing Philippians 4:6.

PHILIPPIANS 4:7

7 And the peace of God, which passeth all understanding, shall keep your hearts and minds through Christ Jesus.

Many people want what verse 7 talks about—but they don't want to practice what verse 6 says to do to get it. *The Amplified* translation of verse 7 says, "And God's peace . . . which transcends all understanding, shall garrison and mount guard over your hearts and minds in Christ Jesus." God's peace will keep guard over your heart and your mind.

But can you reap these results and have this peace without being a doer of the Word? No, you really cannot.

Verse 6 tells us not to fret. People who worry and fret, continually think on the wrong side of life. Verse 8 tells us what we are to think about.

PHILIPPIANS 4:8

8 Finally, brethren, whatsoever things are true, whatsoever things are honest, whatsoever things are just, whatsoever things are pure, whatsoever things are lovely, whatsoever things are of good report; if there be any virtue, and if there be any praise, think on these things.

DO verse 8. *Practice* this verse. Think about the right things. Many people think about the wrong things. You know what they think about because of what they talk about. The Bible says, "*. . . out of the abundance of the heart, the mouth speaketh*" (Matt. 12:34). They continually worry and fret and think on the wrong side of life—and they continually talk unbelief. You cannot be a doer of the Word and continue to talk unbelief. The more you talk about some things, the bigger they get. If something does not meet all of these qualifications—if it is not true, honest, just, pure, lovely, of good report—do not think about it and do not talk about it!

The Amplified translation of First Corinthians 13:7 reads, "Love . . . is ever ready to believe the best of every person." I have found through the years that most of the stories I have heard about people do not even meet the first qualification. They are not even true. So don't talk about the stories you hear. Don't even think about them. Some things you hear might even be true—but they might not be pure and lovely, and notice this—of a good report. Therefore we are not to think about them.

By thinking about such things, we give place to the devil. His greatest weapon is the power of suggestion. He is ever endeavoring to enter your thought life. That is why we are told in God's Word to, *". . . think on these things"* (Phil. 4:8).

Particularly in the Epistles, God the Holy Spirit is speaking to the Church. So meditate on these letters and what He has to say—and be a doer of the Word. You will grow spiritually.

Give the Word First Place

The training, the developing, the educating of our spirits comes by giving the Word of God first place in our lives.

PROVERBS 4:20–22

20 My son, attend to my words; incline thine ear unto my sayings.

21 Let them not depart from thine eyes; keep them in the midst of thine heart.

22 For they are life unto those that find them, and health to all their flesh.

God says in this passage, ". . . *Attend to my words* [Give heed to them—Put them first]; *incline thine ear unto my sayings* [Listen to what I have to say]. *Let them not depart from thine eyes* [Keep looking at the Word of God]; *keep them* [my Words] *in . . . your heart."*

There are rich dividends for doing this. Why is it that God tells us to put His Word first, and to listen to what He has to say, to keep looking at His Word, and to keep His Word in our heart? It is because *". . . they* [His Words] *are LIFE unto those that find them, and HEALTH to all their flesh."*

The margin of the *King James* says the word translated *health* is the Hebrew word for medicine. God's Word is "medicine to all their flesh." There is healing in the Word.

In the 12 years I pastored, there were church members who would get sick, go to the hospital, and then ask for prayer. I am not saying it is wrong to have a doctor, certainly not. We believe in hospitals and doctors. Thank God for them. But I am saying, why not put God's Word first? Sometimes as a last resort, Christians will turn to the Word.

A Baptist minister, who didn't even particularly believe in divine healing at the time, told of how he'd had problems with his tonsils. His doctor kept insisting that they be removed. So the date was finally set for his tonsils to be removed.

It was his family's custom to read the Bible and pray together each morning before the children went to school. On the very day this minister was scheduled to enter the hospital, this family's daily scripture passage was the one which tells of King Asa, who got a disease in his feet and instead of seeking the Lord, he sought physicians and he died (2 Chron. 16:12–13). *Wow!*

The minister said he was struck by this. He realized that he had not even prayed about his tonsils. He shared this with his wife and children and asked that they pray together about his tonsils.

When they prayed, the Lord told him not to have them removed. To his astonishment, the Lord healed the tonsils and he has had no more trouble with them.

There is a lesson to be learned here. The Bible does not imply that King Asa died because he put the physicians first. However, it does imply that he should have put the Lord first. We should train ourselves to put the Lord first.

We should train ourselves to ask ourselves concerning any matter, "What does God's Word have to say about this?" We should ask ourselves what God has to say about anything that may come up in our life—and then put that Word first. *Amen*

Sometimes family and friends will try to rush you into things—but you need to think about what the Word of God says. Put God's Word first in every area of life.

Instantly Obey the Voice of Your Spirit

The human spirit has a voice. We call that voice *conscience*. Sometimes we call it *intuition*, an *inner voice*, or *guidance*. The world calls it a *hunch*. But what it is, is your spirit speaking to you. Every man's spirit, saved or unsaved, has a voice.

The human spirit, as we have seen in previous chapters, is a spiritual man, a spirit man, an inward hidden man. He is hidden to the physical senses. You cannot see him with the physical eyes, nor touch him with your physical hands. This is the man who has become a new creature in Christ (2 Cor. 5:17). When a man is born again, his spirit becomes a new spirit.

God prophesied through both Ezekiel and Jeremiah that a time would come when He would take the old stony heart out of men and put in a new one. He said that He would put His Spirit into us. Under the New Covenant, this New Birth became available.

The New Birth is a rebirth of the human spirit. As Second Corinthians 5:17 tells us, if any man be in Christ, he is a new creature—everything that was old in his spirit, the old nature, is taken away, and all things have become new.

As you give this newborn spirit the privilege of meditating on the Word of God, the Word becomes the source of its information. Your spirit will become strong and the inward voice of your conscience, educated in the spirit, will become a true guide.

Did you notice that meditation in the Word, practicing the Word, giving the Word first place, all come before obeying your spirit? You see, if your spirit has had the privilege of meditating in the Word, of practicing the Word, of putting the Word first—then your spirit is an authoritative guide.

"The spirit of man is the candle of the Lord. . . ." (Prov. 20:27). Your newborn spirit has within it the life and nature of God. The Holy Spirit dwells within your spirit. ". . . greater is he that is in you, than he that is in the world" (1 John 4:4). The Holy Spirit dwells in your spirit. God has to communicate with you through your spirit because that is where He is. Your spirit gets its information through Him.

Learn to obey the voice of your spirit.

If you are not accustomed to doing that, of course, you will not get there quickly. As we have said, your spirit can be built up and strengthened just as your body can be built up and strengthened.

Your spirit can be educated just as your mind can be educated. But just as you did not begin school in the first grade one week and graduate from the twelfth grade the next week, your spirit will not be educated and trained overnight.

However, if you will follow these four points and practice them, after a while you can know the will of God the Father even in the minor details of life. You will receive guidance and will always instantly get either a *yes* or a *no*. You will know in your spirit what you should do in all the affairs of life.

CHAPTER *29*

Praying in the Spirit

For if I pray in an unknown tongue, my spirit prayeth,
but my understanding is unfruitful. What is it then?
I will pray with the spirit, and I will pray with the understanding also:
I will sing with the spirit, and I will sing with the understanding also.

—1 Corinthians 14:14–15

The Lord enlightens us and guides us through our spirits. If that be the case—and it is—then we need to become more spirit-conscious. We need to become more conscious of the fact that we are spirit beings, and not just mental or physical beings. We need to train our spirits so they will become safer and safer guides.

One of the greatest spiritual exercises there is, is to pray in tongues every single day. Your spirit is then in direct contact with the Father of spirits.

I AM a spirit being a mind & body

1 CORINTHIANS 14:2

2 For he that speaketh in an unknown tongue speaketh not unto men, but unto God: for no man understandeth him; howbeit in the spirit he speaketh mysteries.

It is your spirit praying when you pray in tongues—the Holy Ghost gives the utterance, but it is your spirit praying. Paul said, *"For if I pray in an unknown tongue, my spirit prayeth . . ."* (1 Cor. 14:14).

I have always followed the policy of daily praying in tongues. It keeps my spirit in contact with the Father of spirits. It helps me become more spirit-conscious.

When you pray in tongues, your mind grows quiet—because you are not praying out of your mind. And once your mind is quiet, you become more conscious of your own spirit, and of spiritual things.

Get out of the sense realm. Get out of the flesh realm. Get out of the human reasoning realm.

Get over into the faith realm and into the spirit realm. Faith is of the spirit—and that's where great things happen!

We having the same
spirit of faith (2 Cor 4:13)

Characteristics of a Spirit-Filled Life

And be not drunk with wine, wherein is excess; but be filled with the Spirit;
Speaking to yourselves in psalms and hymns and spiritual songs,
singing and making melody in your heart to the Lord;
Giving thanks always for all things unto God and the Father
in the name of our Lord Jesus Christ;
Submitting yourselves one to another in the fear of God.

—Ephesians 5:18–21

[This appendix has been edited from a transcript of Brother Hagin's evening message given on February 18, 2002, during Kenneth Hagin Ministries' Winter Bible Seminar.—Ed.]

In writing to the church at Ephesus, Paul encouraged the believers to *"be filled with the Spirit."* We need to be filled with the Spirit if we're to be led by Him. But many Christians have been confused about what it means to be filled with the Spirit. This confusion comes from a misunderstanding of what the Scriptures tell us about the believers at Ephesus.

Acts chapter 19 tells us the believers in the church at Ephesus had already been filled with Spirit.

ACTS 19:1–2,6

1 And it came to pass, that, while Apollos was at Corinth, Paul having passed through the upper coasts came to Ephesus: and finding certain disciples,

2 He said unto them, Have ye received the Holy Ghost since ye believed? And they said unto him, We have not so much as heard whether there be any Holy Ghost.

6 And when Paul had laid his hands upon them, THE HOLY GHOST CAME ON THEM; and they spake with tongues, and prophesied.

If the believers in Ephesus had already been filled with the Holy Ghost, why would Paul encourage them to be filled with the Spirit in the fifth chapter of Ephesians? The answer lies in the Greek word for *filled*. Greek scholars tell us the word translated *filled* in Ephesians chapter 5 means "a continuous action." So Paul was telling the believers at Ephesus, *". . . BE BEING FILLED with the Spirit."*

You see, there is one initial infilling with the Holy Ghost. That's what we call the baptism in the Holy Ghost, and we see an example of that baptism in Acts chapter 19. But there are many refillings throughout our life. Being filled with the Spirit is not simply a one-time event with a beginning and an end. *It is a continuous, lifelong experience.*

Notice the first part of Ephesians 5:18 says, *"be not drunk with wine, wherein is excess."* Well, people who get drunk don't quit at a sip of wine, do they? No, they keep drinking. In the same way, to be filled with the Spirit, you have to keep on drinking. You have to keep drawing from the Holy Ghost.

How do you draw on the Holy Ghost? You draw on Him by doing what the Word says about being filled with the Spirit. You maintain the characteristics of a Spirit-filled life.

First Characteristic: A Song in Your Heart

One characteristic of the Spirit-filled life is that *you'll have a song in your heart.* Let's look again at a verse from Ephesians chapter 5.

EPHESIANS 5:19

19 Speaking to yourselves in psalms and hymns and spiritual songs, singing, and making melody in your heart to the Lord.

If you are filled with the Spirit, it will be recognizable. People will know it. You'll know it, too, because if you are full of the Holy Ghost, you will have a song in your heart. What does it mean to have a song in your heart? It means you've got joy!

The Bible says, *"For the kingdom of God is not meat and drink; but righteousness, and peace, and JOY in the Holy Ghost"* (Rom. 14:17). If you are full of joy, it will show on your face. You may even dance, sing, or laugh. Sometimes when you're full of joy, you just can't keep from laughing, even when you're by yourself!

So you see, being filled with the Spirit means you'll have joy and a song in your heart. Now, I don't mean some song that you get out of a songbook. The songs we sing in church are fine. We ought to sing didn't have any songbooks back in the Apostle Paul's ... have printing presses back then.

...n is talking about *"psalms and hymns and spiritual songs."* He is describing something that the Holy Ghost gives you. These songs come from your heart, on the spur of the moment. They are given to us by the Spirit to help us.

I've noticed that in the hard places of my life, I find myself speaking in psalms and spiritual songs. In the most severe places, I've spoken nearly all night long in psalms. One night, I actually did speak in psalms all night long. I never slept a wink that night!

During the tough times, the Holy Spirit inspires me. He gives me psalms to help me. Do you remember that Jesus said to His disciples, "I'll not leave you comfortless"? (See John 14:18.) He asked the Father to send "another Comforter," the Holy Spirit. *The Amplified Bible* translates the word *Comforter* as "Counselor, Helper, Intercessor, Advocate, Strengthener, and Standby" (John 14:16). The Holy Ghost is our Standby. He's standing by to help us in the hard places in life. And those psalms He gave me helped me. They were a comfort to me.

Now, read what Paul wrote to the church at Colosse.

COLOSSIANS 3:16

16 Let the word of Christ dwell in you richly in all wisdom; teaching and admonishing one another in psalms and hymns and spiritual songs, singing with grace in your hearts to the Lord.

In Ephesians 5:19, Paul wrote that you ought to be "speaking to yourselves. . . ." In that verse, he's talking about something you do in your own private prayer life. But here in Colossians, Paul says we can be *"teaching and admonishing one another,"* or, in other words, speaking to one another. That means we can speak in psalms, hymns, and spiritual songs at all times. We can do it when we're praying alone. We can speak these songs to another individual. Or we can do it in a public assembly.

But notice the criteria God expects us to meet before we speak! The Word of Christ is to *first of all* dwell in you "richly in all wisdom." Sometimes the Word of Christ dwells in people, but not in wisdom. Paul admonishes you to make sure it dwells in you in wisdom.

Let me give you an example. A number of years ago, way back in 1939, I knew two young men. One of them was 16, and the other one was 17. They got born again and later on were filled with the Holy Ghost.

One day, these two teenage boys went out hunting rabbits. They had a .22-caliber rifle with them. As they headed back home, they walked down a railroad track until they ran into a young boy. Then they stopped, because they wanted to witness to him.

They said to him, "Are you ready to die?"

Well, when this young boy heard what they said and saw that they had a .22 rifle, he took off running!

Later on, these teenage boys said to me, "We weren't going to kill him. We were going to talk to him about Jesus. We wanted to know if he was ready to go to Heaven."

These boys had the Word of God in them. But they weren't using wisdom, so their plan failed. That's why the Word of God needs to dwell in us richly in all wisdom.

The Purpose of Psalms, Hymns, and Spiritual Songs

Notice that Colossians chapter 3, verse 16, goes on to say, "*. . . teaching and admonishing one another.*" How do we teach and admonish others? The rest of the verse tells us we do it *"in psalms and hymns and spiritual songs, singing with grace in your hearts to the Lord."*

Paul means that those psalms would teach and encourage believers. If the Christians in Colosse were facing a test or trial, those psalms they received from the Holy Ghost would teach them or encourage them in what they were going through.

This benefit isn't something that belonged *just* to them. This belongs to every believer! Paul was not writing to just one or two people in those two churches. He was writing to the whole church at Ephesus and Colosse. He was writing to the whole group. And if he was writing to them, then he was writing to us. This benefit belongs to every single one of us!

Now in the Old Testament, no one had the Holy Spirit except the prophet, the priest, and the king. Each of those individuals was anointed by the Holy Ghost to stand in his or her particular office. David was both a king and a prophet. And many of the psalms he wrote were given to him by the Holy Ghost to help him pass a test or trial successfully. In David's hard times, the Holy Ghost gave him a psalm to encourage and teach him.

Speaking Psalms by Faith

We must have faith to step over into the area of speaking psalms from the Holy Ghost. It takes faith to possess anything that belongs to us, and certainly this blessing belongs to us. Speaking in psalms, hymns, and spiritual songs is a means of keeping filled with the Spirit and being blessed.

Psalms come by the Holy Ghost, just like the interpretation comes for an utterance in tongues. When somebody speaks with other tongues, if you're going to interpret, the Holy Ghost anoints you to interpret. But you don't get the whole message before you start interpreting. Usually you will just get the first word or two. The rest of the interpretation comes as you speak out what you already know to say. But you have to start out by faith, trusting the Holy Ghost to give you the rest of the interpretation.

The same is true with psalms. Sometimes I just get a single word. Sometimes I'll get two. Sometimes maybe one line. Then I just start speaking that out by faith.

Here is a psalm that the Lord gave me entitled "Victory."

VICTORY

Victory is not in places.

Victory is not in things.

Victory is in Him, the Eternal One.

For there came One out from the Father long ago—

A Champion into this world,

Given by the Father's love,

Who met the enemy in awful combat.

And He arose victorious over death, hell, and the grave.

And He put the enemy to flight.

So the victory is yours tonight!

These psalms just come out of my spirit. Here is another psalm that the Lord gave me.

WALKING

Walking in the light is walking in the Word.

For the entrance of His Words giveth light.

I'm not in the darkness, but I'm in the light.

Those in the world are in darkness.

Darkness envelops them.

Darkness directs them.

And the enemy of darkness obsesses them.

But I'm in the Light.

And the Light of God shines upon my pathway. Ha, ha, ha, ha.

And I'm full of praise.

And I'm full of joy!

For the Lord is my Light.

Yea, He is my salvation.

He has put the enemy to flight.

The battle is not yours.

The battle is not mine.

But the victory belongs to both of us.

You can see how these psalms would encourage a person in hard times, can't you? Glory to God! That's why we speak in psalms, hymns, and spiritual songs.

Second Characteristic: Giving Thanks

There's another way for Christians to stay filled with the Holy Ghost: *thanksgiving*. Notice what Paul says in Ephesians chapter 5.

EPHESIANS 5:20

20 GIVING THANKS always for all things unto God and the Father in the name of our Lord Jesus Christ.

A second characteristic of the Spirit-filled life is that you give thanks. If you are keeping filled with the Spirit, you are full of thanksgiving. Remember the scripture in Hebrews that says, *"By him therefore let us offer the sacrifice of praise to God continually, that is, the fruit of our lips giving thanks to his name"* (Heb. 13:15). God wants to hear you give thanks.

In connection with this same thought, let's look at a verse from Philippians chapter 4.

PHILIPPIANS 4:6

6 Be careful for nothing, but in every thing by prayer and supplication WITH THANKSGIVING let your requests be made known unto God.

The words *"be careful for nothing"* are a little bit confusing to us. We use *careful* in a different sense than the translators of the *King James Version* did. But the *Amplified* translation helps us. It says, "Do not fret or have any anxiety about anything." Isn't that marvelous? I believe I can do what the Word says I can do, and the Word says, "Do not fret or have any anxiety about anything."

Somebody may say, "Well, if I can't worry, what am I going to do?" The rest of that verse tells you what to do. " . . . *In every thing by prayer and supplication WITH THANKSGIVING let your requests be made known unto God."*

I believe we're way behind with the thanksgiving part. We pray and pray and pray. We ask God for things, or we ask Him for help, and there is nothing wrong with that. But we should also take time to thank God for everything He has done and is doing in our lives. And we should praise Him for Who He is.

Weighed on a Scale

When I first received the baptism in the Holy Ghost way back in 1937, I read the following testimony: A missionary on the foreign field contracted smallpox. This happened before doctors had the smallpox vaccine. Many times the disease was fatal, and it was very contagious, so they isolated this woman to keep it from spreading.

The missionary testified that as she was praying, the Lord gave her a vision. In the vision, she saw an old-fashioned balance scale. One side of the scale was labeled "prayer," and the other side was labeled "praise." She noticed the side for prayer was stacked high, and because of the load, it sank down. On the side for "praise" was just a little stack. As a result, this side was way up in the air.

The Lord said to her, "When your praises equal your prayers, you will be healed." The missionary went on to say, "For two days and nights, I slept very little. I didn't do anything but praise God. I knew I had to do a lot of praising to get caught up."

For two solid days, she didn't do anything but praise and give thanks to God. At the end of those two days, she was completely healed! Every symptom disappeared. Do you see the value of praise and thanksgiving?

When Should I Offer Thanks?

That missionary praised and thanked God, even under dire circumstances. Notice that Hebrews 13:15 doesn't say, "Let us offer the sacrifice of praise to God every once in a while—if we feel like it, if everything is going good, and when we have a pocket full of money." We are to offer a sacrifice of praise *continually.*

And Ephesians 5:20 doesn't say, "Giving thanks every now and then, if everything is going all right." It says, *"Giving thanks ALWAYS for all things unto God."* Now that doesn't mean you thank God for what Satan is doing. You don't thank God for troubles, sickness, or suffering. No, in the midst of what Satan is doing, you thank God for the privilege to believe Him. You thank Him that His Word is true and that He is faithful. You thank God for another opportunity to exercise and develop your faith.

Remember, if you are filled with the Spirit, thanksgiving is going to come out of your mouth. You're going to speak words of thanks. You're not *thinking thanks* but *giving thanks* for all things. Thanksgiving is the fruit of your lips. *Out loud*

There are too many people in the church who are full of griping and complaining, instead of being full of thanksgiving. They've always got something to gripe about. I've heard people say, "They don't let me sing in the choir." Well, they don't let me sing in the choir either. They may have heard both of us, and that's the reason they don't!

Don't be full of griping and complaining. Be thankful and give God praise with the fruit of your lips.

Third Characteristic: Listen to One Another

The third characteristic of the Spirit-filled life is *submitting yourselves* to one another in the fear of God.

EPHESIANS 5:21

21 Submitting yourselves one to another in the fear of God.

22 Wives, submit yourselves unto your own husbands, as unto the Lord.

Many people have taken Ephesians 5:22 out of context and made it say something that it doesn't say. Many believe this verse means the husband is supposed to be a dictator, so to speak, and rule over his wife. Well, in the previous verse Paul said, *"Submitting yourselves one to another . . . ."* Does that mean we're supposed to dominate one another and rule over each other? No!

How to Thank God

Actually, the Greek word translated "submitting" doesn't refer to what people often associate with that word. Paul is not telling people to be doormats to one another. *Thayer's Greek-English Lexicon of the New Testament* says that the word *submitting* in verse 21 means "to yield to another's admonition or advice."[1] The Bible is telling us to listen to and respect one another. In the next verse where it says, "Wives, submit yourselves to your own husbands," it doesn't mean for the husband to dominate his wife. Instead, that verse is speaking specifically to the wives and instructing them to listen to their husbands and respect their position in the home.

We need to understand that when Paul said this, he was talking about situations where both husband and wife are saved—where both are Christians. He's not talking about an unsaved husband and a saved wife. What in the world could an unsaved husband tell of lasting value to a saved wife? While she should honor him as far as his position as the head within the home, she is not to sin for him. If your husband is not saved, obey the Word and pray for him. The Bible does not tell a woman to submit to sin.

No, Ephesians 5:21 says: *"Submitting yourselves one to another in the fear of God."* In other words, listen to one another. Get along with one another.

You know, if you're filled with the Spirit, you're easy to get along with. Those folks who are hard to get along with are not filled with the Spirit. Now, they may have gotten filled with the Spirit at one time. They may be able to go back to some experience they had years ago, but they are not continually staying filled with the Spirit.

---

[1]Joseph Henry Thayer, *Thayer's Greek-English Lexicon of the New Testament* (Grand Rapids, Mich.: Zondervan Publishing House, 1977), p. 645.

When you're filled with the Holy Ghost, you're not hard to. And if somebody says something that you don't like, you don't let it bother you.

One time, I was sitting in a meeting listening to a minister speak, and he made a negative remark about the faith message. Well, my flesh wanted to respond to what he said, but the Bible teaches us to keep the flesh under. So I kept myself under control and said, "Lord, bless him. I'm sure if I talked to him, I'd find out he really didn't mean that the way it sounded."

I kept my ears open to listen to him. And in about 10 minutes, he gave me an answer to a question on a Bible subject that I'd been studying for about 25 years and couldn't find the answer to. Well, what if I had shut him off and quit listening to him because he made a remark about the faith message? I might still be searching for that answer.

God wants believers to be led by the Spirit and to show forth the characteristics of a Spirit-filled life. Remember, to live a Spirit-filled life, we need to listen to one another; speak to ourselves in psalms, hymns, and spiritual songs; and give thanks. When we do these things, we'll stay filled with the Spirit. We'll walk in the blessings of God. And we'll find it easy to be led by the Spirit.

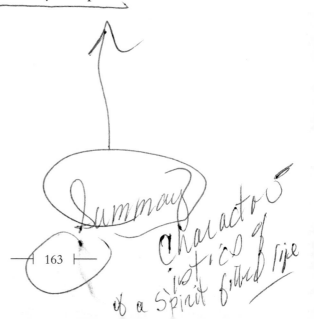

Being Led by the Spirit of God in Prayer

Praying always with all prayer and supplication in the Spirit, and watching thereunto with all perseverance and supplication for all saints . . . .
—Ephesians 6:18

[This appendix has been compiled and edited from transcripts of morning messages Brother Hagin preached during All Faiths' Crusades in Lakeland, Florida, January 22, 2003, and Murrieta, California, March 10 and 11, 2003.—Ed.]

In teaching on the subject of prayer for more than 50 years, I have always used two texts: John 15:7 and Ephesians 6:18. There are no better texts than these for teaching on the subject of prayer, because they are all-inclusive. Anything you want to know about prayer is found in these two verses.

Notice what Jesus said in John chapter 15, verse 7:

JOHN 15:7

7 If ye abide in me, and my words abide in you, ye shall ask what ye will, and it shall be done unto you.

That's a marvelous text, isn't it? It tells you how to get your prayers answered every time: *"If ye abide in me, and my words abide in you . . . ."* You see, if you pray according to the Word, your prayers will work. So many times, we're not praying according to the Word. We're in the dark if we don't know what the Word says. But the entrance of God's Word gives light (Ps. 119:130).

Take time to meditate on the Word until it gets in you. Then, you'll ask what you will, and it shall be done for you.

Praying in the Spirit

The other verse I like to use when I teach on prayer is Ephesians 6:18. Paul wrote this letter to Spirit-filled Christians at the church of Ephesus.

EPHESIANS 6:18

18 Praying always with all prayer and supplication in the Spirit, and watching thereunto with all perseverance and supplication for all saints . . . .

The Amplified Bible translates the first part of the verse this way: "Pray at all times (on every occasion, in every season) in the Spirit, with all [manner of] prayer and entreaty." What does it mean to pray in the Spirit? In First Corinthians chapter 14, we have instructions on this subject.

166

1 CORINTHIANS 14:2

2   For he that speaketh in an unknown tongue speaketh not unto men, but unto God: for no man understandeth him; howbeit in the spirit he speaketh mysteries.

"He that speaketh in an unknown tongue" is talking to God. Well, that's prayer, isn't it? One definition of prayer is fellowshipping with the Father. Therefore, Paul is talking about prayer here. The second part of the verse says, "For no man understandeth him; howbeit in the spirit he speaketh mysteries." Paul is talking about praying in the Spirit. He's talking about praying in tongues.

The last part of the verse tells us that a person who prays in the Spirit "speaketh mysteries." What does that mean? Well, the mystery isn't with God, because God knows everything. The mystery is with us. We don't know everything. Often, we don't know how to pray for a situation unless the Lord shows us or gives us revelation. We don't know what to pray for as we ought. But thank God, the Holy Ghost knows. He will help us pray if we'll allow Him.

Being Led by the Spirit in Prayer

Many of us haven't taken advantage of being led by the Spirit in prayer. Sometimes we run out of things to pray in English. After a while, we've said everything we know to say. If we stop at that point, our prayer life will be limited by what we know. But remember, God knows everything. He knows what we don't know. He wants to help us pray. And praying in the Spirit will get the job done when nothing else will.

Let's look at what First Corinthians chapter 14 tells us about praying in the Spirit.

1 CORINTHIANS 14:14

14 For if I pray in an unknown tongue, my spirit prayeth, but my understanding is unfruitful.

In this verse Paul says that if we pray in an unknown tongue, our spirit prays. *The Amplified Bible* says, "My spirit [by the Holy Spirit within me] prays." In other words, it's the Holy Ghost Who gives utterance to my spirit, but it's my spirit that actually does the praying.

You see, it isn't all my spirit, and it isn't all the Holy Spirit. It's both of them, working together. The Holy Spirit gives our spirit utterance, so we can pray out of our spirit, not out of our head. That's what it means to be led by the Spirit in prayer.

We need to learn to be led by the Spirit! And praying in other tongues provides a way for you to pray for things that you wouldn't otherwise know needed prayer. Look again at Ephesians chapter 6, verse 18.

EPHESIANS 6:18

18 PRAYING ALWAYS WITH ALL PRAYER AND SUPPLICATION IN THE SPIRIT, and watching thereunto with all perseverance and supplication for all saints . . . .

Greek scholars tell us that according to the original Greek manuscripts, the first part of this verse literally says, "praying, *being led by* the Spirit."

Of course, that phrase includes the idea of praying in tongues, but it also means the Holy Ghost will lead you in how to pray. He may lead you differently at different times. Although two situations may look the same, the Holy Spirit may lead you to pray one way one time and another way another time. We may not always know why He's leading us to pray a certain way.

The important thing is to follow the leading of the Spirit. He'll show you the best way to pray concerning your situation. Look to Him to lead you in how to pray in every instance. He'll lead you in the right direction.

Why Do We Need to Pray?

Some people may ask why we need to pray. They may be thinking, "God already knows everything. Doesn't God already know what I need?" Yes, He does know. But you still need to pray. Let me explain why.

At the time of Creation, God made the world and the fullness thereof, the silver, the gold, the cattle on a thousand hills, and everything that's here on earth. Then He made His man, Adam. And God said, "Adam, I give you dominion over all the work of My hands." Adam had dominion over the whole world (Gen. 1:26–28).

But Adam committed high treason. He sold out to Satan. And the Word of God tells us in Second Corinthians 4:4 that Satan is the god of this world. How did he get to be the god of this world? When Adam committed high treason, he gave his dominion to Satan. Satan is dominating in this world because Adam sold out.

Thank God, Jesus came and restored us to dominance. Why, then, do we need to pray? I'll give you three references that at least imply our need to pray.

In Matthew chapter 6, verses 5 through 15, Jesus is teaching on the subject of prayer. Look at what He said in verse 8:

How Sutan got power

MATTHEW 6:8

8 . . . your Father knoweth what things ye have need of, before ye ask him.

Well, if your Heavenly Father knows what you need, why doesn't He just send it? Why would you have to ask Him? Verse 8 makes it clear that Jesus expects us to ask the Father for what we need. This scripture implies that God will not send what you need unless you *do* ask Him.

Now look at Matthew chapter 9. Here, again, Jesus is giving instructions on the subject of prayer.

MATTHEW 9:35–38

35 And Jesus went about all the cities and villages, teaching in their synagogues, and preaching the gospel of the kingdom, and healing every sickness and every disease among the people.

36 But when he saw the multitudes, he was moved with compassion on them, because they fainted, and were scattered abroad, as sheep having no shepherd.

37 Then saith he unto his disciples, The harvest truly is plenteous, but the labourers are few;

38 Pray ye therefore the Lord of the harvest, that he will send forth labourers into his harvest.

I want to ask you a question. Who does the harvest belong to? Is it God's harvest? Yes! Is He the Lord of the harvest? Yes! Does He want laborers? Yes!

If He wants laborers, why doesn't He send them? What need would there be for us to ask Him if He wants to send them anyway? Yet Jesus clearly tells us that we are to pray to the Father to send laborers. This scripture implies that God will not send them unless we ask Him.

Now, look at these verses from Matthew chapter 18.

MATTHEW 18:18–19

18 Verily I say unto you, Whatsoever ye shall bind ON EARTH shall be bound in heaven: and whatsoever ye shall loose ON EARTH shall be loosed in heaven.

19 Again I say unto you, That if two of you shall agree ON EARTH as touching any thing that they shall ask, it shall be done for them of my Father which is in heaven.

Notice that Jesus is telling us to do something here on earth. He's telling us to pray. You see, something has to happen on earth before Heaven moves. Verse 19 tells us what has to happen on earth: "If two of you on earth shall agree as touching anything they ASK." They have to ask! They have to pray!

Praying Through

There must be action on the earth before Heaven moves. So you can see that the Holy Ghost is looking for people who have dedicated themselves to prayer. We sometimes call these people "prayer warriors." People who give themselves to prayer often sense the Spirit of God moving throughout the earth as He tries to find somebody He can use to pray things out!

Why? Because somebody's got to pray about it. Somebody has to pray it out! Do you know what I mean by "praying something out"?

The old-time Pentecostals called this practice "praying through." When you have what some people call a leading—when you have an urge or burden to pray—what do you do? You pray! And when you don't know what you're praying for, you pray in tongues, speaking mysteries, speaking divine secrets as First Corinthians chapter 14 tells us.

"Praying through" simply means that you keep praying until you have a note of victory. What do I mean by a note of victory? Well, after you've prayed for a while, you'll begin to laugh or sing to yourself in tongues. You see, a while ago, you had this burden. You felt this heaviness. Then you prayed. And suddenly, you feel as though the burden is gone. You have a sense of gladness. Those signs tell you that you have prayed the situation through and have the victory!

The Importance of Praying Through

When you have a burden or leading to pray, it's important to yield to that leading and pray until you've prayed through. When you do, you'll experience victory.

Years ago, I read the testimony of a missionary named Brother Boley in a Full Gospel magazine. Later, I had the opportunity to hear him preach in a church in Dallas. In his message, he reiterated his testimony.

Brother Boley and his wife went out as missionaries to Africa in the early 1920s. They went inland, into the very heart of Africa, and built a mission there for a native tribe.

One day, a neighboring tribe kidnapped a six-year-old girl from the tribe he was ministering to. Brother Boley knew the customs of the local tribes. He said, "We knew that if we didn't get the little girl back before sundown, we would never recover her. I got a native man who was saved and could speak the dialect of that tribe. And we went over there.

"Before we got there, we could smell this awful smell. They had a custom of taking an animal and killing it. Four or five women of the tribe had to prepare it. Then, they'd hang this animal on a pole at the entrance to the tribe's land. Everyone who came in had to take a knife, cut a piece off that meat, and eat it. If you didn't eat, the women who had prepared the meat would be killed."

In that hot, humid climate, the meat had putrefied. Brother Boley told his interpreter, "We'll have to eat a bite of that. We don't want those women to be killed. Jesus said, 'One of the signs that'll follow believers is that if they drink any deadly thing, it'll not hurt them.' I supposed that we could also eat any deadly thing, and it would not hurt us. So we said, 'In the Name of Jesus.' Then, we cut a chunk off that rotten, putrefied meat. We each ate a bite, and it never affected us in any way.

"We made a deal with the chief of that tribe," Brother Boley said. "We traded him a bunch of trinkets and beads and things for the girl. But then night overtook us."

Because it was dangerous to travel the jungle at night, Brother Boley and his interpreter stayed overnight in the tribe's guest hut. At midnight, they were awakened by the sound of drums. The interpreter told Brother Boley, "That means we're dead. That's the death knell. It's dawned on the chief that they don't have to give up the girl. They can just kill us and take her back."

The two men heard the tribe members moving around outside the hut. Knowing they were about to die, they committed themselves into God's hands and then stepped outside. Brother Boley said, "I shut my eyes and waited. I know it was just a few seconds, but it seemed like a long time. Nothing happened.

"I heard strange sounds, and when I opened my eyes and looked, the warriors were on the ground! And they were bowing up and down, their knives laying on the ground!"

Brother Boley asked his interpreter what the warriors were saying. The man responded, "They're worshipping you. They think you're a god. They say that when you stepped out of the hut, two giant men in white apparel with a giant sword in either hand stepped out right beside you."

Thank God for His deliverance! But that's not the end of the story. There's more to it.

Soon after his miraculous deliverance, Brother Boley went to check on a lady who was manning a missions station for another local tribe. When he arrived, the woman asked him, "Brother Boley, did something happen to you last Monday night about midnight?"

He said, "Why do you ask?"

"Well," she said, "I always work 14 to 16 hours a day, and I was very tired that Monday, so I got to bed and went to sleep. I was awakened with a burden to pray. I lay there in bed and began to pray. But I was so sleepy, I fell back to sleep. I was awakened again. And I had the same burden to pray! So I prayed, but I was so weary that I fell back to sleep. I was awakened the third time about 10:30 that night, and I decided to get up because I knew if I lay there, I'd go back to sleep."

The woman got out of bed, got on her knees, and said, "Lord, I don't know what it is you've awakened me to pray for. I don't know who it is who needs prayer. I just trust the Holy Ghost to give me utterance." And she began to pray in other tongues. She prayed approximately an hour and a half in other tongues.

"While I was praying," she told Brother Boley, "your face kept flashing before me. I don't know whether I was praying for you or not. At midnight, I knew I had prayed through. I began to laugh. I began to laugh in the Spirit and sing! The burden lifted. Instead of a spirit of heaviness, I felt a spirit of lightness."

The night she prayed was the same night Brother Boley was delivered from death. It was a mystery to her why she was awakened to pray, but it wasn't a mystery to God! What if she hadn't prayed? Thank God, she did!

You can see the necessity of following that leading to pray, even though we don't know what it is we're praying for. Afterward, we sometimes find out what we were praying for. Sometimes, we'll never know until we get to Heaven. But how important it is that we respond to the Holy Spirit when He leads us to pray!

When the Spirit Leads You to Pray—Pray!

I want to share with you an experience from my own life of a time when I was led by the Spirit to pray.

Back in 1979, we began holding Prayer and Healing School on the RHEMA campus. The musicians would sing a little bit, and we'd take up an offering. Then, they would turn the service over to me. Often, I would stay in a room by myself and pray before coming out to take over the service.

One day, I came walking into the little auditorium where we held Healing School. As the offering was being received, I sat down on the platform. Suddenly—that's the way the Holy Ghost moves—suddenly, you know, this burden came on me to pray! And I thought, "I have to pray, and I have to pray *now*. Somebody's life is in danger. Somebody's near death." I just sensed in my spirit that someone, I didn't know who, but someone was near death.

I got up and said to the crowd, "Folks, I've got to pray and pray now. I have this burden. I have to pray, so let's pray now." I knelt down to pray, and I'll tell you, by the time my knees hit the floor, I was in the Spirit. I mean, I was praying in tongues. And I prayed earnestly for at least 45 minutes.

And then, I got a note of victory. I began to laugh. I began to sing quietly to myself. Praise God! I knew that whatever it was, and whoever it was, I had the victory.

At 9:30 that night, I got a telephone call from a young lady whose mother had been a great supporter of this ministry for many years. Around 3 o'clock that afternoon, there had been an explosion in the Texaco Refinery in Port Arthur, Texas, and the young lady's father was caught in there with 17 other men. Six and a half hours had come and gone. The men were still trapped, and the firemen had not been able to put the fire out. They were in fear for the lives of all those men.

This young lady was calling to ask me to pray. I started laughing right on the phone because I suddenly realized who I had been praying for earlier that day. I said, "There's no need to pray at this point. I already got the victory on that. I already got it! He's all right. Your father's all right."

My wife and I got off to bed, and at 1:30 in the morning, the phone rang. We had two phones, one by each of us, so we both answered.

It was the same young lady. She told us, "Momma just called. They finally got the fire put out, and they got in there, and they can't believe it. All 18 men are safe." Hallelujah!

Can you see why it's so important to pray when the Spirit leads you to pray? What if I hadn't prayed? I got the whole group at Healing School to pray with me. What if we hadn't yielded to the Spirit? Those men could have died!

Learning to pray when the Holy Spirit leads us would avert many dangers. If Spirit-filled believers would follow His promptings and become prayer-conscious, many problems wouldn't happen.

Many terrible things would never happen if folks were really led by the Spirit.

Great Things Happen
When We Pray in the Spirit

Being led by the Spirit does more than avert trouble in our lives. It also helps us usher in wonderful moves of God. Great and mighty things have happened in the past, as God's people have prayed. And great and mighty things are going to happen more and more. But they're not going to come just because God decides, "Well, I'm going to bless this one. I'm going to bless that one."

No! They will come as a result of our praying!

Back in 1942, I was the pastor of a church in East Texas. Toward the end of November of that year, I'd get up between 2 and 4 o'clock in the morning, Monday through Friday, and go into the living room to pray for an hour.

Now, I wasn't led to do that. Sometimes you're led. Sometimes you have a leading, a burden, to pray in certain ways and along certain lines. But I would simply pray in English to begin with. And I'd say:

"Lord, we thank You for all the gifts and manifestations of the Spirit: the three revelation gifts—the word of wisdom, the word of knowledge, and discerning of spirits; the three power gifts—faith, working of miracles, and gifts of healings; and the three vocal gifts—prophecy, divers kinds of tongues, and interpretation of tongues.

"Lord, we have an ample manifestation of the vocal gifts. We never have a service that doesn't have a tongue and interpretation. We have an ample manifestation of revelation gifts. But it seems to me that there ought to be more manifestations of these power gifts: faith, the working of miracles, and gifts of healings. And so I pray that there will be a greater manifestation of these gifts than we've seen before."

Now, in about 15 minutes, I had said everything I knew to say in English. I'd be finished praying what my mind knew to pray. So I'd say, "I trust the Holy Ghost Who is living inside me to give me utterance to pray about this and anything else that God wants me to pray about." And I'd spend the rest of the hour praying in tongues.

I did that day after day, five days a week, week after week, from the last two weeks of November down to the 23rd day of February, 1943. That's over three months! And on the 23rd day of February, the Lord began to talk to me.

He said, "At the close of World War II, there will come a revival of divine healing to America." Well, that revival started in 1947, and it became the easiest thing in the world to get people healed. I learned later that other people were led by the Spirit to pray in that direction. We had no communication with one another and didn't know we were all praying for the same thing. But thank God, He answered our prayers.

Persevering in Prayer

I believe that the same kind of breakthrough can happen today if we'll just stay in prayer until we have the victory.

EPHESIANS 6:18

18 Praying always with all prayer and supplication in the Spirit, and watching thereunto with all perseverance and supplication for all saints . . . .

What is perseverance? I heard one fellow call it "stickability." Just stay with it. Stay with praying until you've prayed through. I think that many times, if something doesn't happen fast enough, we give up too soon. And if we give up, we won't see the results God intends for us to have.

I'm reminded of a story I heard about the East Texas oil field. Much of the oil has been pumped out through the years. But back in the late 1930s, it was thriving. A man in the oil business there had made a million dollars and then lost it. A bank was financing him so he could drill another well. The money ran out, and he still hadn't hit oil. But he was convinced that if he could go just 50 feet deeper, he would hit oil.

One way or another, he talked the banker into extending a little bit more money. He drilled 50 feet farther down and hit a gusher. It made him a multimillionaire overnight.

Well, what if he'd quit? What if the bankers had said, "No, we've given you all we can give you. That's it! That's the end of it." But they drilled just a little farther and hit a gusher.

I think sometimes if we'd just pray with a little more perseverance, if we'd just be more determined, we'd have greater manifestations of the gifts of the Spirit. We'd see great and mighty things happen!

How to get answered prayer.

Being Led by the Holy Spirit in Ministry

". . . The Lord seeth not as man seeth; for man looketh on the outward appearance, but the Lord looketh on the heart."

—1 Samuel 16:7

[This appendix has been compiled and edited from transcripts of messages Brother Hagin preached during Kenneth Hagin Ministries' Campmeeting in Tulsa, Oklahoma, the evenings of July 28 and 30, 1988.—Ed.]

In 1943 and 1944, I was pastor of a small church in Farmersville in north central Texas. One Mother's Day, I'd been asked to speak at another church at a special Sunday afternoon service. That meant I had to miss the morning service at my own church. So, we told our church that we'd have our Mother's Day service that evening. (We had the largest crowds in the evening services, anyway.) Since it was

May, it was warm enough that the windows and doors were open, and sometimes we had more people outside than inside.

I'd worked for weeks on my Mother's Day sermon, and it was a good one, too—what we used to call a "stem-winder." I had my notes, I had scriptures, and I had quotes from Benjamin Franklin, Abraham Lincoln, and others. I was ready.

During the service, some of the youth and children gave a recitation about mothers and every song honored mothers. Everything was about mothers.

As I sat there while a trio of young ladies sang the last song before I was to preach, the Spirit of God said to me, "As soon as they get through singing, get up and have a healing service."

I said, "Dear Lord, they'll think I'm nuts. This is Mother's Day. Don't you understand? There's been nothing said about healing. The whole service has been about mothers." I never did know what that trio was singing, because I was having an argument between my head and my heart. (You see, the Spirit of God doesn't dwell in your head. He dwells in your heart, in your spirit. He doesn't speak to your head. He speaks to you in your spirit—in your innermost being.)

I looked over the crowd. Several men there had come only because their children were part of the program. I thought, *These men won't be back in church until Christmas. I can preach about mothers and get a little sentimental, and they might come forward and get saved.*

When the time came for my sermon, I stepped up to the pulpit, pulled out my notes, and read my text. But I couldn't go any further. I closed my Bible and said, "Folks, I have to obey God." And we had a *powerful* healing service!

An older man in the congregation could not walk upright. When I laid hands on him, the power of God hit him and straightened him up immediately. He bent over backward and touched the floor. He bent over forward and touched the floor. He went through all kinds of gymnastics. Normally, a man his age—he was about 69—couldn't have done that. When other people in the congregation saw it, they were encouraged, and they started getting healed!

I looked toward the back and saw all the men who had come to see their children—the ones I thought would never be back if I didn't preach about mothers. They were sitting there weeping. God had touched them. He knew how to reach them. And many of those men came back the next week!

A lot of times, we preachers think we know what needs to happen because we've got our program all arranged. The Holy Spirit will try to move in a service, but He can't because we're trying to push our program.

Now, having a sermon outline is good. And staying with it is all right if it's necessary. But if the Holy Ghost leads you to do something else, do it! Have you ever noticed that sometimes God doesn't work in ways we think He ought to? We'd like it if God told us His whole plan from the start, wouldn't we? It would be a lot easier on our flesh and minds if He did.

The Prophet Samuel had to deal with this issue when the Lord told him to anoint a new king of Israel. Let's look at part of the account in First Samuel chapter 16:

1 SAMUEL 16:1,4–13

1 And the Lord said unto Samuel, How long wilt thou mourn for Saul, seeing I have rejected him from reigning over Israel? fill thine horn with oil, and go, I will send thee to Jesse the Bethlehemite: for I have provided me a king among his sons. . . .

4 And Samuel did that which the Lord spake, and came to Bethlehem. And the elders of the town trembled at his coming, and said, Comest thou peaceably?

5 And he said, Peaceably: I am come to sacrifice unto the Lord: sanctify yourselves, and come with me to the sacrifice. And he sanctified Jesse and his sons, and called them to the sacrifice.

6 And it came to pass, when they were come, that he looked on Eliab, and said, Surely the Lord's anointed is before him.

7 But the Lord said unto Samuel, Look not on his countenance, or on the height of his stature; because I have refused him: for the Lord seeth not as man seeth; for man looketh on the outward appearance, but the Lord looketh on the heart.

8 Then Jesse called Abinadab, and made him pass before Samuel. And he said, Neither hath the Lord chosen this.

9 Then Jesse made Shammah to pass by. And he said, Neither hath the Lord chosen this.

10 Again, Jesse made seven of his sons to pass before Samuel. And Samuel said unto Jesse, The Lord hath not chosen these.

11 And Samuel said unto Jesse, Are here all thy children? And he said, There remaineth yet the youngest, and, behold, he keepeth the sheep. And Samuel said unto Jesse, Send and fetch him: for we will not sit down till he come hither.

12 And he sent, and brought him in. Now he was ruddy, and withal of a beautiful countenance, and goodly to look to. And the Lord said, Arise, anoint him: for this is he.

13 Then Samuel took the horn of oil, and anointed him in the midst of his brethren: and the Spirit of the Lord

came upon David from that day forward. So Samuel
rose up, and went to Ramah.

Why didn't God tell Samuel, "Go anoint David"? Why go through
the elimination process? Why did God tell Samuel who the next king
wouldn't be instead of who he would be?

Samuel was as human as the rest of us. He was trying to make a
logical choice among Jesse's sons. He thought the oldest must be the
one. But the Lord told Samuel, *"Look not on his countenance . . . for the
Lord seeth not as man seeth; for man looketh on the outward appearance, but
the Lord looketh on the heart"* (v. 7). If the Lord looked on our outward
appearance, a lot of us would be in a mess.

Once, while holding meetings in Kansas, I spent an afternoon
alone in prayer about the meetings. During that time, I began thinking about my personal faults and failures, and mistakes I'd made in the
past. As I did, I got embarrassed. I said, "Lord, I'm almost embarrassed
to stand in your presence." Then I started listing occasions when I had
made mistakes or missed His direction in different circumstances.

His response startled me. His Voice was as real to me as if someone
were standing in the same room with me. I even looked around to
see if someone was there. He said, "I know you missed it. But I was
looking on your heart all the time. I wasn't looking at the outward
man." That's when He showed me First Samuel 16:7. He continued,
"Even though you've made mistakes, your heart has always been right
toward Me." That blessed me!

So as Samuel observed each of Jesse's sons, God kept saying, "No,
not him." I imagine Samuel started to wonder if he had missed
God in going to Jesse's house. So he asked Jesse, "Do you have any
more sons?"

Some people think prophets know everything. But that's not the
case. We as ministers don't know everything, either. All we know is

what God tells us. Often during a service, God has told me there's someone present He wants to minister to. A few times He has also told me who it is. But that's the exception, not the rule. Samuel knew only what God had told him—that one of Jesse's sons would be the next king of Israel.

Why doesn't God tell us the whole story all at once? *Because if He were to tell us everything about our situations, we'd be walking by sight and not by faith. And if we don't walk by faith, we can't please Him* (Heb. 11:6). That's the reason He didn't tell Samuel at the start which of Jesse's sons to anoint as king.

The pianist in our church in Farmersville had a tumor in her left lung as big as a man's fist. She hadn't asked us to pray, and she hadn't gotten in a healing line. But as I concluded the service one Sunday morning, the Lord told me, "There's a woman here I want to heal before you go today."

Now if I had hesitated, I would have thought, *Well, if there's a woman He wants to heal, doesn't He know who it is?* I would have dismissed the service and missed God. And this dear sister might not have received her healing.

Before I had time to think, I said, "The Lord wants to heal a woman here this morning."

A lady stepped out of the congregation and started walking toward the front. In my spirit—in what we call the still small voice—I heard, "She's not the one." So I said to this woman, "Sister, you're not the one He's talking about. But come on down, because healing belongs to you. I'll pray for you and lay my hands on you."

About that time, the pianist stepped out. The Holy Spirit said to me, "She's the one." So I laid hands on her and prayed.

The following Tuesday, she went back to the hospital for treatments. After a few X-rays, the doctors told her the tumor was completely gone!

You see, God wants us to walk by faith. He will lead us one step at a time, and each step requires faith. Sometimes, we think he's leading us in one direction based on the last step He told us to take. But actually that step was to position us to go in another direction. Pastors, evangelists, and laymen—*all of us* need to understand this principle.

How God Led Us to Tulsa, Oklahoma

[In Chapter 11 of this book, Brother Hagin relates how the Lord let him know that He wanted him to move his offices to Tulsa, Oklahoma. Here, Rev. Hagin provides further details of that move.—Ed.]

The Lord had told me that He wanted us to move our offices to Tulsa and that He would give us Brother T.L. Osborn's former office building. A while later, He awakened me one morning at sunrise and told me to go see a certain businessman in Tulsa. Now, I knew this man had money, but I wasn't about to ask him for money. I'd never asked anyone for money personally, and I wasn't about to start.

So, Oretha and I drove to Oklahoma City on business. While we were there, I called this businessman and we agreed to meet him and his wife for dinner in Tulsa. So we met them, and had dinner. I never said anything to him about moving to Tulsa or what God had told us about Brother Osborn's building.

As we left the restaurant with this couple, another couple, long-time friends (he later became one of our board members) drove up to have dinner at the same restaurant. They shook hands with the couple we had just eaten with, and then that couple got in their car and left. Then the couple who had just arrived invited us to eat with them. We thanked them for the offer but said we had just had dinner.

"Well, come and drink a glass of tea or something," they said. So we went back into the restaurant with them.

While we were talking, I said (almost jokingly) that we might move to Tulsa into T.L. Osborn's old offices. The man spoke briefly with his wife, pulled out his checkbook, and handed me a check for $1,000 to help us make the move.

"Oh, no, no, no," I said. "We're just thinking about this. We probably won't do it."

The man said, "Take it. God's been talking to us about giving you that money. Use it for whatever you want."

"In that case," I said, "I'll take it. Thank you."

Before we left Tulsa, we went to a shopping center to buy a few things. While we were there, I saw a man I had met through the Full Gospel Business Men's Fellowship. Again, I mentioned in passing that we might move to Tulsa.

He said, "We'll give you $1,000 toward your move."

I had to call another man I knew, and I mentioned about Brother Osborn's building, and he said, "Put me down for $1,000."

When we got back to the house where we were staying and told that couple what was happening, the husband said, "Put me down for $1,000."

Within a few days, I had spoken with a couple of other businessmen about the move and the finances already offered. They each said, "Put me down for $1,000."

Before I knew it, I had $7,000 either in hand or promised in support of our move to Tulsa. God just put that together. It was the easiest thing in the world.

My point is that if I had never gone to Tulsa to meet with the man God told me to meet with—the one who *didn't* give us money at that time—I wouldn't have run into that second couple who *did* give us money.

Many times when God leads us, things don't go the way we think they will. But we need to let God lead us step by step, and walk in faith.

Don't Be Ashamed to Back Up

In 1951, I was preaching in Oklahoma at a regional meeting for a Pentecostal denomination. At the end of a particular session, the Lord told me to call a certain businessman to the front and lay hands on him, and He would fill him with the Holy Ghost. I knew this man. He was well known in the community, but he wasn't Pentecostal. He was a member of a Nazarene church.

As well known as this man was, I didn't want to call him out by name. So I said, "If anyone wants to be filled with the Holy Spirit, come down to the front, and I'll lay hands on you, and you'll be filled with the Holy Ghost."

Two or three came down, but the businessman did not. I came off the platform and laid hands on those who responded. But it was like laying hands on a doorknob. Nothing happened. No one got anything spiritually, because I had missed God. He didn't tell me to call everyone down. He told me to lay hands on a specific person.

So I backed up. I returned to the platform and told the people, "Folks, I missed God. I need to back up. Forgive me." I then called this man down to the front, and before I was actually able to lay my hands on him, he threw his hands up and started speaking in tongues!

Too often, we ministers are so afraid of admitting that we've missed God that we continue down the wrong path rather than backing up, making the correction, and moving on. As you minister, if you feel like you've lost the anointing, don't be ashamed to back up and correct yourself!

Being Led by the Spirit in the Operation of Spiritual Gifts

Often, while I'm praying over an evening service, the Lord gives me no particular direction for my message. In fact, He has said, "Don't spend time getting together a sermon. Just wait on Me. Whatever is needed in the service, I'll pull it up out of your spirit." You see, I've been putting the Word into my spirit for all the years I've been in ministry, just like you put things into a computer. So the Lord has something He can draw out. That's why many times I don't know which direction the service is going until the singers are through with praise and worship.

Now, I'm just as human as you are, and I'd like to know ahead of time what the Lord wants to do in a service. Many times, He doesn't let me know. But the Holy Spirit lives in me, and I trust Him to give me what's needed for a particular service.

In relation to that, let's consider the following verse from First Corinthians chapter 3:

1 CORINTHIANS 3:16

16 Know ye not that ye are the temple of God, and that the Spirit of God dwelleth in you?

We've emphasized the fact, and it's scriptural, that God's Spirit dwells in us individually. But we need to understand more fully that it is also true that God's Spirit dwells in us collectively—in a local congregation, in a meeting, and in the whole Body of Christ. God's Spirit dwells in every believer individually, and in every body of believers collectively.

Solomon built a *physical* temple or house for God in the Old Testament. Today, we are *spiritual* dwellings of the Spirit of God. And since we are spiritual beings and houses, we need spiritual gifts.

As I traveled from church to church early in my traveling ministry, I noticed that I was able to operate in the spiritual gifts in some churches more than in others. In one church, I would prophesy or have a word of knowledge. In other churches, as many as seven of the nine gifts or manifestations of the Spirit mentioned in First Corinthians chapter 12 would be in evidence. But in some churches, I wouldn't do anything but teach.

Finally, I asked the Lord, "Why is this?"

He took me to First Corinthians 14:1, where Paul encouraged the church at Corinth to *"desire spiritual gifts."* He then told me that this epistle was not written to an individual person. Rather, it was written to a whole group of people collectively. Paul was telling the whole church body at Corinth to *desire* spiritual gifts. And if they would desire them, the Holy Spirit would distribute the gifts to individuals among the congregation as He willed.

The Lord told me that in order for spiritual gifts to manifest in a church, that church must first believe in spiritual gifts, and then they must desire them! (Here again, we see the truth of Hebrews 11:6 that without faith, it is impossible to please God.).

People need to know more about spiritual gifts. When they see what God's Word says about spiritual gifts, they can believe in them and receive the benefits of those gifts operating in their lives.

The Leading of the Holy Spirit

People have asked me what I mean when I say that I have a leading of the Holy Spirit to minister to an individual. Well, the best way I can explain it is like this: imagine a string tied to your spirit, not your body, that's pulling you in a particular direction. During a time of ministry, you'll feel as though that "string" is pulling you toward someone.

This has happened to me many times. When I get to that person, I lay hands on them. Although I may not know any specific information about the person or their situation, when I lay hands on them, I know exactly what the problem is.

Another method the Spirit of God uses to lead me is by giving me what I call a "mini-vision." Sometimes before a service or time of ministry, in my spirit, I'll see myself doing something such as laying hands on a particular person or praying for a situation. When the time comes in the service, I'll do what I saw myself do in that vision.

Jesus operated in a similar way.

JOHN 5:19

19 Then answered Jesus and said unto them, Verily, verily, I say unto you, The Son can do nothing of himself, but WHAT HE SEETH THE FATHER DO: for what things soever he doeth, these also doeth the Son likewise.

The Local Church's Role

We need to understand that Jesus Christ, as the Head of the Church (His Body), wants to do the same thing through His spiritual body that He did through His natural body. That's why He needs you.

The Apostle Paul said, *"Now ye are the body of Christ, and members in particular"* (1 Cor. 12:27). Christ is the Head. We're the Body. This refers to the universal Church. Every born-again believer is a member of that Body. But when a local group of believers meets together, they, in effect, become a body of Christ. They become a temple— God's sanctuary.

Look at this verse in the *Amplified* translation of First Corinthians chapter 3:

1 CORINTHIANS 3:16 (*Amplified*)

16 Do you not discern and understand that you [the whole church at Corinth] are God's temple (His sanctuary), and that God's Spirit has His permanent dwelling in you [to be at home in you, collectively as a church and also individually]?

We as individuals are temples for the Holy Spirit, but when we come together locally, we collectively become a temple of God for that meeting. Too often all eyes are on the preacher in a service. However, there is great power in a group of believers in agreement.

We've seen a lot of people in wheelchairs delivered. There were three in one night. No one laid hands on them, but the Glory of God was present. They jumped up and started walking. Some people say, "Oh, I wish we'd have more of that." We could if congregations would hook up spiritually with the minister. Doubt and unbelief in a congregation can hinder the work of the Holy Spirit. Jesus encountered that in Mark chapter 6.

MARK 6:1–6

1 And he went out from thence, and came into his own country; and his disciples follow him.

2 And when the sabbath day was come, he began to teach in the synagogue: and many hearing him were astonished, saying, From whence hath this man these things? and what wisdom is this which is given unto him, that even such mighty works are wrought by his hands?

3 Is not this the carpenter, the son of Mary, the brother of James, and Joses, and of Juda, and Simon? and are not his sisters here with us? And they were offended at him.

4 But Jesus said unto them, A prophet is not without honour, but in his own country, and among his own kin, and in his own house.

5 AND HE COULD THERE DO NO MIGHTY WORK, save that he laid his hands upon a few sick folk, and healed them.

6 And he marvelled because of their unbelief. And he went round about the villages, teaching.

Jesus was able to do no mighty work in his own hometown because the people did not believe. So, what did He do? The same thing we as ministers should do—*teach.* As people's understanding of the operation of the Holy Spirit increases, their ability to believe in those manifestations increases, and so does their ability to receive. No pastor, minister, evangelist, or prophet can do more than the congregation will let him do.

When I was ministering in Oklahoma one time, a 72-year-old woman who had been confined to a wheelchair for four years came down during the healing portion of the service. Three of the best doctors in the state had examined her and said she would never walk again. Before I could lay hands on her, she started crying out loudly.

"Wait a minute, sister," I said, "I have a word from God for you." The Spirit of God inspired me to say that. But she continued wailing at the top of her lungs. Every time I tried to quiet her down, she just got louder—yelling at the top of her voice. She sounded like a freight train going through a tunnel. Finally, I stood right in front of her and hollered, "I command you in Jesus' Name: shut up!" She finally calmed down. Why did I do that to a 72-year-old woman? I had to be louder than she was to get her attention. With all of her yelling, she couldn't hear that God had something for her.

Now the congregation didn't understand what I was doing. They thought I was being rude to the woman. So they unhooked spiritually. I couldn't minister to that woman because the congregation had put the brakes on.

So I stopped and spent a few minutes teaching—explaining to the congregation what I had just done. Many of them understood and lifted their spiritual feet off the brakes. I could actually sense it in my spirit. And the service moved forward. *In less than 10 minutes,* that dear woman who the doctors said would never walk again started leaping and jumping all over the front of the church, totally healed! But if I hadn't been able to get enough people in the congregation in agreement with me, I never could have ministered to her.

In my field ministry meetings, I was used to seeing 60 percent or more of the people healed—and sometimes nine people out of 10. But in one meeting, I knew that not even 10 percent of the people were being healed.

I went to God about it. I fasted and prayed a couple of days. And I asked the Lord where I was missing it. The Lord said, "It's not you. There's too much unbelief in the crowd. You won't see anybody get healed there." Then He reminded me of several instances when He had to change the surroundings before He could minister healing to someone. One instance was in Mark chapter 7:

MARK 7:32–35

32 And they bring unto him one that was deaf, and had an impediment in his speech; and they beseech him to put his hand upon him.

33 And HE TOOK HIM ASIDE FROM THE MULTITUDE, and put his fingers into his ears, and he spit, and touched his tongue;

34 And looking up to heaven, he sighed, and saith unto him, Ephphatha, that is, Be opened.

35 And straightway his ears were opened, and the string of his tongue was loosed, and he spake plain.

The Lord asked me, "Why do you think I took him aside from the multitude?"

"I don't know," I said. "I always wondered."

The Lord said, "I couldn't heal him in that multitude. There was too much unbelief there."

Now, it's different when you are in a place, on the mission field for example, where there's no local congregation putting the brakes on. But for the most part, local church congregations in America know enough that their faith affects the success of someone trying to pray for the sick. In churches that were consistently taught about spiritual gifts, I always have complete freedom to minister as God leads me.

A Word From the Lord to Ministers

The time is now. The day has arrived. You're already on the edge of it.

Now, walk on. Do not look back. Make the necessary dedication and consecration.

Walk on. Walk in the power of God. Minister in the power of God.

And all that I've said unto you will surely come to pass. None of it will fail, for the Lord has decreed it. The Lord has ordained it for these last days.

And because it is the time of the end times and certain things have been fulfilled, other things will shortly be fulfilled—fulfilled in the natural world and fulfilled in your own life and ministry.

And it shall come to pass at last, and thou shalt rejoice and be glad.

For the Lord has spoken, and no demon, devil, or Satan himself, and certainly not humankind, will be able to stop it, for the Lord is moving.

Get
How to train your
human spirit
CD !
136